PENGUIN BOOKS

THE EX-FILES

After being thrown out of her marital home with just the clothes on her back and Rs 750 in the bank, Vandana rebuilt her world and founded the first Indian support group to help people going through a divorce, 360 Degrees Back to Life. She has since come full circle from being a litigant to being a divorce lawyer and practices at the family court in Mumbai. Currently, Vandana's work for the cause of women going through divorce in India has resulted in a BBC documentary about her work, titled, *Invisible Women of India*. This was broadcast worldwide on International Women's Day in 2014.

Vandana writes a monthly column in the magazine, *Black and White*, Oman and she edits *Ex-Files*, India's first divorce newsmagazine. She has also participated in the Lead India Programme and was one of the eight finalists from Mumbai. Her work has been extensively covered in the media in India and the Middle East. Her first book, *360 Degrees Back to Life: A Litigant's Humorous Perspective on Divorce*, endorsed by the iconic feminist Gloria Steinem, won an award. Vandana has translated another book on the Jain faith from Hindi to English.

Coming from an armed forces background, Vandana Shah grew up in Ambala and moved to Mumbai as a teenager. She studied at St Xavier's College in Mumbai and has since donned various hats including that of a model, a deejay and an advertising professional.

PRAISE FOR THE BOOK

'Champagne-dripping, solitaire-studded, a Jimmy-Choo-on-steroids, divorce memoir that lightens the trauma of divorce . . . that you just can't put down'

—Advaita Kala

'Finally, a divorce we can laugh and cry at. Through a silver rendition of her story Vandana let's it all hang. It's succulent, simmering and complex. Just like the paneer makhani she swears by!'

—Arif Zakaria

'Vandana's book carries forward where Vatsyayana left off, a bold and timely treatise on "sex and Kamasutra in divorce"—stunning and unputdownable'

—Padma Vibhushan Dr Sonal Mansingh

'When Holy Wedlock becomes Holy Deadlock, what do you do? Cry your heart out or laugh it off? Here is a book which will help you to enjoy your way through the thickets of divorce and plot the second marriage. Read, relax and rejoice'

—Padma Bhushan Lord Meghnad Desai

The EX-FILES

THE STORY OF MY DIVORCE

VANDANA SHAH

Sdé

Shobhaa Dé
BOOKS

An imprint of Penguin Random House

SHOBHAA DÉ

USA | Canada | UK | Ireland | Australia
New Zealand | India | South Africa | China | Singapore

Shobhaa Dé is part of the Penguin Random House group of companies
whose addresses can be found at global.penguinrandomhouse.com

Published by Penguin Random House India Pvt. Ltd
4th Floor, Capital Tower 1, MG Road,
Gurugram 122 002, Haryana, India

Penguin
Random House
India

First published in Shobhaa Dé Books by Penguin Books India 2014

Copyright © Vandana Shah 2014

All rights reserved

10 9 8 7 6 5 4 3 2

The views and opinions expressed in this book are the author's own and the
facts are as reported by her which have been verified to the extent possible, and
the publishers are not in any way liable for the same.

ISBN 9780143418580

Typeset in Bembo by Ram Das Lal, New Delhi
Printed at Manipal Technologies Limited, India

www.penguin.co.in

MIX
Paper | Supporting
responsible forestry
FSC® C043100

This is a legitimate digitally printed version of the book and therefore might not
have certain extra finishing on the cover.

To the people who have helped me spread my wings
and fly, spreading love and light in the world:
You are a princess . . . so said my parents
You are the queen of my heart . . . so said
(I wish) Rafael Nadal
You are spiritual . . . so said my Buddhist guru, Tsugla
Lopen Samten Dorji, my Jain saint brothers, Shri Prem
Muni, Mukesh Muni and others including Sadhviji Sunita
and Radha Soami Satsang Beàs's Gurinder Singh Dhillon
You are special . . . so said Shobhaa Dé
and Gloria Steinem
You will become me . . . so said the work of
Aung San Suu Kyi and Oprah Winfrey

Contents

Contents

Foreword

I have known Vandana as a student—then I lost track of her till we met years later. Her marriage was fractured and she was going through an ugly divorce. Yet she was not sad or depressed—in fact, as is her wont, she was bubbly and smiling! She had just written a book, detailing her travails and though dealing with a serious subject, there were doses of humour in it. But behind that façade was a tinge of pain. The book was read at a couple of events which I attended and initiated discussion. I continued to meet Vandana infrequently—she kept in touch and I learnt about her trips abroad as a public speaker. So I am glad she has now come out with a well-documented novel. It is definitely autobiographical and brings out the pathos and problems that she underwent for over a decade. It certainly takes courage to write such a personal book and that is what it is all about—straight from the heart and head. The divorce went through and she found love again, hence it is only apt that the 360 degrees (her first book) now completed, she is sharing her experiences and thoughts and more importantly reaching out to others in distress. It is a sort of catharsis for her and yet there is so much to learn as she delves into the recesses of her life. It is not facile to confront the truth and be candid about the anguish, but she has dealt with it honestly and passionately. It is evident she has grown over the years and the trauma of marriage and divorce has emboldened her to divulge the 'other side' of matrimonial bliss (sic) in India. The hypocrisy and sham that camouflage many a marriage in this country are sharply brought out. Then there is a passing reference to the ignominy of being single, divorced, widowed for an Indian woman and the social prejudices that stem from this portrayal. Indeed the book would be a lesson in learning to cope with the vicissitudes of life for the readers as they will undergo a vicarious experience of caring and sharing *The Ex-Files*.

There is no bitterness and rancour as Vandana takes on life on her own terms—a saga of courage, determination and hope—the way to go ahead.

Professor Nandini Sardesai,
September 2014

Prologue

The Times of Yesterday
20 MARCH 2001: Fair, lovely, convent-educated, married, served with a shocking divorce petition

The Times of Money
20 MARCH 2003: Fair, lovely, convent-educated, in the divorce court, living pennilessly

The Times of Depression
20 MARCH 2006: Fair, lovely, convent-educated, going through depression

The Times of Delay
20 MARCH 2007: Fair, lovely, convent-educated, still in the divorce court

The Times of Hope
20 MARCH 2008: Fair, lovely, convent-educated, maybe getting the divorce after all

The Times of Champions
20 MARCH 2009: Fair, lovely, convent-educated, innocent, divorcee looking for . . .

Is this how my matrimonial advertisement would read, I wondered. It sounded like an advertisement for a product, the only difference being I was pre-owned, born-again single, or realistically speaking, second-hand in the marriage market.

I never meant to write this book. But when I was, completely inexplicably, served with a divorce petition, the situation arose. I say inexplicable because I had no idea that my marriage was in a state to warrant an untimely death. It was inexplicable because I never thought I would have to go through a divorce. inexplicable because I thought divorce happened in movies, and not to small-town girls. Inexplicable, because I thought divorce was a fate reserved for 'fast girls' and not God-fearing ones like me. Inexplicable, because I thought I was done with the courts after the fight for my father's estate where I accompanied my widowed mother who battled it out like a warrior to win the case. Inexplicable, because I thought all such negative things happened to others, and not to me. Inexplicable, because I didn't understand the machinery that accompanied the entire process of my divorce. Inexplicable, because I still don't know why this happened to me.

After all the pain, hurt, humiliation and the jarring exposure to a harsh reality, I still say inexplicable.

At the most fundamental level, there is a really difficult question—what does divorce mean? There are so many distinct elements of divorce, it almost seems as if divorce is a living entity. The tongue of divorce is perhaps people's tongues talking endlessly about you; its hands are your hands despairingly calculating the legal expenses which are like the high tide and your earnings which are like the low tide. The legs of divorce are your legs running away from the court; the eyes are the eyes of people staring and watching every move you make; the internal organs are the strength you need to tell your intimate bedroom stories in a divorce petition; the brain whose workings we are clueless about is the stigma of divorce.

Sometimes, I wonder whether we, in India, are living in the twenty-first century, or if we are a developing nation, at all. You only need to hear the whispers, or the 'Oh!' mid-conversation, accompanied by an infinitesimal pause, followed by the feeble attempts to change the topic to understand the stigma attached to divorce in India. One only has to ask the many journalists who try and write articles about divorce and eventually have to can them because they can't get interviewees to disclose their names. No one wants to talk about divorce and much less, be identified by it. Turn on the television and how many programmes do you get to see on the subject of divorce?

When I questioned a supposedly progressive television channel about why this was so, all they had to say was that the idea was ahead of its times. Because, you see, no sponsor will come forward for anything on divorce because they don't want to appear as though they are encouraging the idea. This is extremely illogical because it does not take a TV show to break up a marriage. Instead, it is only when the decay has set in that you turn to TV programmes and other sources for guidance and succour.

The shockingly sad part is that the situation was exactly the same about ten years ago. And when I listen to the hushed whispers surrounding divorce ten long years later, the voices mutter the same thing. It's like a big carpet thrown over the entire story of divorce. The muffled voices below are talking about the denial of breakdown of a marriage, finances, society, parents, the fight over the children, the fear of the divorcee tag.

Why am I going on and on about the ten-year time period? That's because my 'situation' with getting a divorce lasted ten years and nothing much has changed. I was married for two–three years but getting a divorce took me ten years. Even now when I talk about it, people are still shocked and gasp about how long it took for my divorce to come through and how open I am about it. I'm not saying that you need to declare your relationship status from the rooftops but we need to at least acknowledge that divorce exists and it is happening. With the changing sociological structure in India, divorce is like that unwanted houseguest that no one wants but is here to stay.

It is because of the stigma associated with divorce that there is also an abysmal lack of public support about it and you are forced to completely trust lawyers and kind-hearted strangers in the state divorce machinery because even your family is split wide open between whether they will or will not help you. The help, if any, comes in trickles weighed down heavily with the baggage of expectations and biases. The lawyers, then, can easily take you for a ride if they so desire. I know because my first lawyer did take me for a bad bumpy ride. In fact, even in the divorce support group that I initiated, once a case was resolved, a number of the people just did not want to be associated with the cause. Some of them even stopped taking my calls—it was like they didn't want to be identified as divorcees because it was akin to having a fatal, contagious disease. A friend who worked in a foreign consulate once summed it up by saying, 'Talking about divorce in India is like taking on the cause of AIDS about a decade ago because of the tremendous stigma. Tough galvanizing action is required to bring about any changes.'

I look at the books on divorce in the Indian market and they are incredibly complicated, research-based books written in dry, factoid forms, or the books are third-person accounts. I haven't seen any *divorcologue* (I made that word up and after this book, you never know, it might just get included in the dictionary!) in India. There is no book which shares the experience of divorce in its entirety—complete with the legal aspects, the sociological cycle, the socio-legal aspects as well as psychological facets, which are all interlinked, and laced with humour for brightening an otherwise dismally depressing experience, compounded by stigma.

This is the most compelling reason for me to write a book on divorce which is not only honest and humorous, but also serves as a guide and holds a mirror to society. I don't want vulnerable people to suffer, I'd rather they learn from my experience and not make the same mistakes I made. This book runs a gamut of emotions from humour, joy, ecstasy, pain, negativity, positivity and, of course, survival and winning. It's our story coming true. It's about you and me. It's about remembering that divorce can happen to anyone and it shows no discrimination.

This is not a blame-all book, nor is it a hate-all book where I point fingers at my former in-laws and husband. That would not only be hitting below the belt (which is not my style or philosophy) but would also make the book very, very boring. I would add that my ex-husband's family is extremely wealthy—some would call them the liquor barons of the country. They are educated and have a good name in society. Should I tell you more about them? I'm not going to because they aren't worth it and I don't want to portray them as villains and me as the heroine who was a damsel in distress—no judgements please. So they are in the trigger point for this book but are peripheral in my life.

I have been told that this book is a brave effort and I am very gutsy. I don't know about all these tags but it is a story that needs to be told and that's what I have done—as honestly as possible, hoping this will change the attitude of people. Even if it changes only one person's point of view, it would be the start of a cultural shift.

1

Divorce Walls

I was no longer in Kashmir or on the LOC. There was no more dispute or status quo. I was free to go skinny dipping, date whoever I wanted, become a sanyasin or even the President of the country if I wanted to. My mind, floating to a different level, wondered—does make-up conceal pain—as I stared at the damp, dank divorce walls. I had coined this term for the walls of the family court. After all, when you spend a lot of time with anyone or anything, you have affectionate names for them. So why not for the divorce court? I also felt that such names were needed given that I was dealing with an excruciatingly painful life-altering situation, somewhat like the false humour and sense of well-being exuded by visitors to a terminally ill person. And then I put on my natural make-up—a twinkle in my eyes, a smile on my face, hope in my heart and a lilt in my step—and was ready to face, if all went well, my ex-husband.

I couldn't believe I had thought of the phrase 'if all went well'. Wasn't that supposed to be associated with a happy event? Subconsciously, my heart had spoken the truth and had quieted my logical mind which kept coercing me to feel sad because this was the end of a marriage—the relationship was on the funeral pyre and the pyre was about to be lit. I was glad I had listened to my heart while getting dressed in the morning and had worn, after many years, my light blue jeans—waist size 26 (of course I'm lying about the size but a white lie to keep myself happy is a small thing!)—a white sleeveless top and my old big, blue Guess handbag, blue eye pencil and no lipstick.

This was revolutionary dressing in comparison to my divorce courts uniform, worn at the behest and orders of my various lawyers and reflecting my dead, dull and tragic life—a dreary, white bag-shaped kurta, worn with a slip, white scarf and an unfashionable *pyjami* which made me look ten years older, and like a widow in mourning. A widow I would soon be but of a different kind. Let's just say I was a modern-day widow.

'Vandana B, Vandana B,' a loud nasal voice shrieking out my name broke my reverie. It was the court peon summoning me. This shriek had grown on me and did not bother me any more, unlike the first time I had heard it and it had felt like a train was rushing through my ears and heart and shredding them into a million pieces. But by now, I had become immune. So I smiled at the peon, who, over the years had become a friendly, caring acquaintance. He would offer me a seat when the courtroom was crowded and I was physically exhausted from all the endless waiting. He'd even offer me tea when I was depressed with the entire goings-on over which I had no control.

I was, by now, a divorce veteran but was I always like this? Why did this have to happen to me and what had brought me to this juncture of my life? I was leading a fairly simple and uncomplicated life before it all exploded. So many questions but unfortunately, the answers, explanations and justifications just didn't add up. Would they ever, I wondered?

'Vandana B, hurry up. Your turn has come,' the voice shrieked again which forcibly evicted these thoughts from my mind and made me concentrate on the present moment. I saw my divorce lawyer, a kind-looking woman who had transformed my life, smiling at me and calling me to a corner in the court. 'Hi! I'm glad our turn has come early today because I'd like us to finish soon.' I laughed inwardly at the joke. Soon? After all these years of waiting, we were now rushing through to save five minutes.

I knew that this was not the time for these thoughts so I told my inner voice to shut up and wore my natural make-up yet again. This time, I wore a smiling, attentive face and responded excitedly, 'Yeah, let's hurry up. Where are they? Are they coming or backing out? I don't see them. Have you seen them?'

She said, 'Hey, slow down with the questions. Yes, they are here. In fact, they got here before us and seem very eager.' I replied, 'Great!' And to which she said, 'Don't be nervous, it'll all go well.' This was, I was sure, the stock line that all lawyers use to calm clients down.

She then said, 'You look different . . . aah! It's your clothes—you aren't wearing your usual court clothes. You look nice in jeans.' I knew she was changing the topic but a compliment is a compliment and especially one about your looks always makes you smile. 'Thanks,' I said, grinning at her.

Then I saw the opposite party, looking in my direction. He looked the same—tall, fair, good-looking. He was wearing blackish grey trousers, a blue pinstriped half-sleeve shirt and black polished shoes. He was dressed as though he was going to the office. He probably was too—after this thing got over. This thing, this 'disruption' and inconvenience in his picture-perfect disciplined life. I subconsciously pushed the hair back from my face and adjusted my handbag to look well-dressed for him. Would that change his mind about this? He just stared at me and I attempted a feeble smile in his direction, trying to be civil and courteous.

He quickly looked away as you do when you see a maimed beggar, scrounging at your car window. You don't want to make eye contact because you are not inclined to help. The beggar's condition is neither your concern nor your business, and you can't bear to look because making eye contact binds you in a moral obligation which you have no intention of fulfilling. The opposite party was my husband and the thing was our divorce.

There. I had said it. Straight and to the point, instead of using euphemisms like separation, working things out, not getting along, and giving each other space. Yes, we were here for our divorce, for the final goodbye, to seal our fates without each other. If we slept with each other after this, would it be considered immoral? I chuckled to myself, as we would no longer be bound in holy matrimony. After all, isn't marriage somewhat legalized prostitution? No, it isn't, I checked my mental sarcasm, bordering on cynicism. Marriage is a beautiful, holy union of minds where two people come together and pledge to spend the rest of their lives together and be honest and committed to each other in good times and bad. Then what really is divorce? Does it have a clear cut definition except the one provided by the Oxford dictionary, which says that divorce is 'the legal dissolution of marriage'. Does this definition cover all aspects of divorce? Is divorce as simple as its definition? Before I could continue further with this soliloquy, I realized my lawyer was signalling to me and calling me towards her.

Both of us, my husband and I, then made our way silently to just outside the counsellor's office with our emotional and financial bodyguards, our lawyers. I wished either one of us would speak instead of pretending that all was well and we had come together to sign a simple lease deed. As I looked around, I thought we could possibly talk about the helpless people with sad eyes waiting their turns in court. A few people seemed happy but they were in a minority. I wished that we'd talk about the clerks in their white government uniforms with expressions that only government officials have—an expression that clearly said, 'I know what is going on but I can't do anything about it. I am not corrupt and will never do anything out of turn unless, of course, the right opportunity turns up.' Instead, the deafening silence between us continued and the clerk who seemed like he had read my thoughts told us to enter the counsellor's office.

Just as we were about to enter, a couple went in before us and I thought, 'It's a sign from the heavens that the divorce is delayed and perhaps cancelled even. After all, if an arrest warrant can be cancelled, then why not a separation?' Suddenly, I noticed the couple had been escorted out and my friend, the clerk, was grinning sheepishly at me, speaking in Hindi and translating into his local version of English saying, 'Madam, you go first. Your case has been going on for a long time. I have told the other couple to come later.'

I just stared at the clerk, my eyes filled with a silent gratitude and wonder. This can only happen in India, I thought, this absolutely lackadaisical attitude to one person's time but a striking contrast of a caring attitude towards someone who they perceive as the underdog or maybe towards someone they like or a million reasons which you may or may not be privy to. I think this kindness bias towards the underdog is a universal phenomenon but is all the more evident in India where people are very expressive both in their words and actions.

So we were ushered into the counsellor's office. Usually,

when you enter a room, you get the 'vibes' of the room, but today seemed different. The air in the office was heavy and had an indecipherable quality to it, like it had too many secret stories to share and was exhausted by sharing them.

I took in the surroundings—rickety chairs, plastic flowers, rexine handbag belonging to the counsellor, important-looking law books, a good view as all government offices have. It was also as shoddily maintained as all other government offices. As I smiled at my lawyer, since the opposite party would not smile at me, my eyes went up to the white calendar, designed with gaudy roses and plump children desperately trying to look endearing and gasped audibly looking at the date—20 March 2009.

I realized that the room looked the same as it did a decade ago. A decade seems interminable but I can't believe that a decade has gone by . . . and my mind does back fillips and cartwheels to the time when it all began.

2

Holy Moley—It's Happening

Underweight in my underwear. It has a nice ring to it, I thought, admiring my reflection in an itsy-bitsy white thong, its sheer satiny lace band hugging my teeny weeny waist in the mirror. Finally! At last, I had accomplished my goal of being below the recommended weight for my height and age, at least once in my life. Vital statistics are an important concern for a young girl and at this time, they had taken the cutting, obsessive edge of a competitive athlete—like a Florence Joyner on steroids.

All I could think about was how many calories a slice of watermelon had and if I ate a single slice of bread, how I would cross over to the other side of, well, not being skinny any more. I definitely did not want that at this stage of my life. After all, this was barely a month away from the penultimate day of my existence so far.

Was it a life-changing day, I sometimes wondered idly. Well, since everybody said it was, it must be so and with the entire buzz around it, I also began to believe that this day defined my very being. Everything else I had done till now would pale in comparison to this. Every single action would be measured against this landmark and from what I had heard, read and seen it sure seemed like that. This single day would be a game changer for me. It would define the rest of my life. All my mistakes until now would be nothing, because after this day, they would be forgotten.

Whether I had done well in school, college or even my job, nothing would matter. In fact, even if I had committed murder, that act would also somehow not matter. All my previous dalliances with other men would also be forgotten and looked upon indulgently as a passing phase with a great emphasis on how 'nothing really happened' which is why there was no need to bring them up and they were safely discarded to the black hole of family memory. Anything before this would be part of another life whose only purpose was to somehow surreptitiously, cunningly and slowly but surely prepare me for this.

Oh yes, this was the D DAY—3 December, the day I was to get married.

I was getting married, so my entire life was going to be newly forged. It seemed akin to growing a new skin. So my life before that, plainly put, was really nothing. All my accomplishments before this—getting university ranking grades, a foray into modelling and deejaying, being a sportsperson, a good daughter, a loyal sister, a good friend, a kind human being, a charitable and well-informed individual—just didn't add up to much when measured against the benchmark of not just getting married but into a wealthy family to boot. In fact, being an individual was not important and certainly not encouraged in the period running up to the marriage. Conformity was the name of the new chapter.

Marriage in India is the ultimate culmination of your dreams and life and marriage to a guy from a 'good family' (which basically meant a wealthy family) is more important than achieving your dearest dream. With only thirty days left for 'the day', I was trying to look bride-perfect, even if it meant saying goodbye to food. Days and days were spent shopping, preparing my trousseau, meeting friends and some relatives, albeit reluctantly. I also managed crucial logistics, which otherwise would have been managed by my parents, like choosing and sending the wedding invites, the venue, the menu and the financials involved in these, which were setting me back by a fortune.

Quite often, at the end of a long day, I would be dog-tired and in two minds about whether all this running around was worth it. One part of me would say, 'You are giving up a part of your life *and* spending money like water to do it? Why go through all this madness?' Another part, which I am sure was my heart, would cry out breathlessly, 'You will be a princess for a day. The entire world's attention will be focused on you, and your to-be husband will be the prince who will carry you off into a fairy tale.' My heart can only have been influenced by the many romance novels I had read because I strongly believed in the happily-ever-after. What a contradiction we are—modern-day women guided by pragmatism and yet hoping for storybook perfect lives.

An important part of the day, leading up to the marathon marriage madness, was also the romancing that happened on the phone when we shared our daily lives and they seemed so important. Any time the phone would ring and the familiar number would flash, my heart would skip a beat, my face would curve into a smile and my eyes would sparkle like the diamonds in my engagement ring. The kisses on the phone would seem inadequate and would only add to the impatience of wanting to do the real thing. Of course, these lovey-dovey conversations were packed with so many sweet nothings. We put our best foot forward and never said anything mean or rude and never ever got angry or abusive towards each other. We spoke of hope and how we would, as a couple, rule the world. And no matter how tired and lonely I was, these calls were an instant pick-me-up and added more to my anticipation of the prospect of marriage.

My thoughts often wandered to my deceased parents. They, my mother especially, would have been happy that I hadn't chosen unconventional professions like modelling that I was doing as a hobby and had chosen matrimony over a professional career. Mom would also be 'extra' happy since I was settling into a well-off family. My mother was so focused on my getting married that I felt like I was a part of a Jane Austen novel. According to her, money did take away a lot of pain that you suffered and my father would tease her mercilessly for this attitude of one panacea for all ills. My father would be glad that I completed my education and was financially self-sufficient. He would also be happy that I was marrying a well-educated boy. I bet they would both cry a lot when the actual *bidaai* (send-off) would take place.

My parents were an omnipotent presence in my life and occupied the top most rung in my heart. I always spoke of them, especially my father, in such loving and glowing terms that a guy I had just met said, 'Hey, I'd really like to meet your father. He sounds like such a nice person!' I swallowed hard and said, 'Ah, he's actually no more.' The guy looked confused and said, 'Oh, I'm sorry! The way you were speaking about him, I thought he was still around.' I gulped in embarrassment as I realized that I was speaking about my dad in the present tense even though I had lost him to cancer when I was very young. I was sixteen and the dark day indelibly etched in my memory was 22 November.

I still remember him lovingly calling me 'Dolly', especially when I was angry with him and sulking. He would pamper me and I fully believed him when he said I was his princess. But being an Air Force pilot, he did what could only be called measured pampering because there was always a huge emphasis on being disciplined and doing well in school by being an all-rounder. This is what prompted me to excel in academics and extracurricular activities in school. He looked so regal when he was in his uniform—tall, big built and always so well dressed. My father was also an Olympic level cyclist and had competed in the Asian Games. I was so proud of my dad being in the Air Force that for the longest time if anyone would ask me his name, I would rattle off, 'Wing Commander Sanwal Shah.'

I was very lucky that my dad was in the Air Force because he could spend so much time with me when I was growing up and we travelled the length and breadth of the country. In hindsight, I realize that it is the best gift that he could have given me and that it shaped my personality. He insisted his daughters read the newspaper and learn five new words a day. He instilled self-sufficiency in me and that I would grow up to be a working girl. Every time my mother said, 'She's a good looking girl and girls don't have to work once they are married. Vandana will certainly get married to someone from a rich family. Why do you insist on her working?' My father would reply, saying, 'Even if that is so, she must still be financially independent.' He really was a feminist and my first real exposure to one.

In fact, all three of us sisters were very proud of our dad and loved him to bits. I'd like to think that my dad indulged me a little bit more because I was the youngest of three sisters. The age gap between my oldest sister and me being over seven years, which really feels like an eternity when you are in school. Maybe this was the reason why it was impossible to be close to my sisters interwoven with all other factors like distance (they moved out of India) or just so many other reasons that the families conceal and shrug off. Being the youngest, you are always bullied by your older siblings but are also spoilt by everyone in the family. It seems like a fair trade-off to me—bullied and loved the maximum!

One incident involving my father that stands out clearly in my mind has shaped my thoughts and a major portion of my personality. As a child, I would come from Ambala to my grandmother's home in Mumbai for the summer holidays. My cousin, the grandson of the house, used to get extra mango milkshake and I really wanted extra milkshake too. I asked him one day about why he got extra, he said that it was because he was a boy and boys get extra because they are better than girls.

I disagreed but he said everyone at home also said the same thing. I told him that they were lying because girls and boys are equal and my father had said so. We fought quite a lot over it, finally ending the conversation with me punching him and calling him names, forcing him to agree with me. In fact, I even wrote a long letter to my father after this incident to which he replied and said that both boys and girls are equal but ended by saying that I must not demand more in someone else's house and I was definitely not to hit and punch my cousin. And so, I grew up thinking that both genders are equal, which is very progressive thinking in a country where the birth of a girl child is greeted with sorrow even to this day.

Mom was, well, mom—she was like all the moms in the world. She was so pretty and wore such nice clothes that I would always open her cupboard when she was not there and look at her beautiful clothes. I would drape and feel her silk and chamois satin sarees against my skin. The drawers in her cupboard always had her lipsticks and I would open the cover and see their colours but there was never any nail polish. You see, she used to bite her nails and so she never painted them. Mom was pragmatic and ambitious and encouraged me to strive for the best and spent so much time feeding me that I can still feel the effects. She was an amazing cook and made the best non-vegetarian food, even though she was herself a vegetarian. So really dinner time was the best time when all of us would sit around the dining table eating Mummy's food and chat about the events of the day and usually Dad and Mom both would give us solutions to any problems we had.

Mom was always there for me, magically solving all my problems, and giving me so much time and unconditional love that I believed I could achieve anything that I wanted. She instilled an unflinching faith in me about my abilities and would laud my achievements without ever putting any pressure on me. So the goal that was set out for me was to do well without ever crumbling under pressure.

I did well in studies, so she never had any complaints. In fact, during my second year of college, she sat me down one day and said, 'Your life is your own but if you spoil your own life by not thinking through your actions, you will have to bear the consequences. I am too old to be spying on you and too sick to follow you around, giving you moral lectures (MLs I used to call them). If you don't get married because you have a bad reputation, it will bother me for some time but not enough to kill myself over it. I was married to a great man and only you will suffer alone for your antics, because eventually even I will die.'

I took this advice in the right spirit because I knew she

meant well. In fact, I once overhead her describing me to a friend, exhorting her to find a boy for me. My mother described me as 'tall, beautiful, intelligent, doing very well academically'. What warmed my heart was hearing her say that I was a loving, caring daughter and there was nothing more a prospective husband or mother-in-law could ask for.'

Her advice has stayed with me through all the good and bad times. I made my own life and carried myself with dignity. I still miss her terribly especially when I have a gossipy secret to share which I can't confide in anyone else. Although I have a treasure trove of memories of both my parents the reality remains that I am an orphan (how I hate that word) and I was made to feel it all the more acutely, not only when I was about to get married but also throughout my marriage.

My parents were very much in love and were quite demonstrative about it as well. My father called my mother 'darling' or Charan—he hardly ever used her name. I do not remember Mom and him fighting beyond the usual minor quarrels. In fact, he used to tease Mom playfully about having a crush on the actor Sanjeev Kumar and she used to respond by saying that Dad was always number 1 in her life. I grew up in a home filled with unconditional love, laughter, open-mindedness, coupled with gentle discipline. I lacked nothing. I knew that both my parents loved me and so I was only focused on doing well academically and becoming someone in life.

I didn't, however, enjoy their love for very long. I lost Dad to cancer when I was sixteen. I still remember his strong athletic body ravaged by this killer disease and till the end he kept trying to battle it out but lost finally. After his passing, Mom and I were by ourselves as my sisters were married and living with their husbands abroad. We moved to Bombay after Dad's death because Mom was a Bombay girl and had spent her childhood and gone to school and college in Bombay. Her side of the family and some of her friends also lived here. There were some complications relating to Dad's estate and Mom bravely contested and won those cases. I used to occasionally accompany her to the court, but she mostly fought it out alone and won. My poor brave mom was diagnosed with cancer a few years after Dad and also died when I was in my twenties, before I could get married. Nothing can explain or compensate the loss of parents but I constantly make peace with it by uttering platitudes to myself.

I was ambitious and after my mum passed on I took up a job and was faring quite well and earning well. My mother had left me some money and a small flat in Santa Cruz and I was not terribly rich but was well off which was now being used for my marriage expenses. My know-it-all relatives said to me, 'But this expenditure has to be done because it is expected from the girl's side.' They also thought that I must have done some great karma to be getting married into such a wealthy family, especially when I had almost reached my sell-by date. Boys go for younger girls and I wasn't exactly a nubile nymphet because I was twenty-six years old, and to top it all, I had no parents. It had to be destiny. Trust relatives to always prick your balloon of happiness.

When you are twenty-six years old and have lost both your parents to cancer and have no brother, getting married becomes somewhat of a task because of the social expectations that go with a marriage. After all, if there are no parents then who will the elders from the opposite side talk to? Who will take the responsibility for the girl? Who will stand guarantee for the girl's behaviour? Whose house will she go to when she is pregnant? Who will perform the ceremonies that are centred on the presence of the parents or a brother? The weighty question also remains— who will undertake the expensive and laborious logistics of marriage, the ceremonies before the marriage, the actual ceremony and the ceremonies after the marriage. There are so many details involved in a wedding for which you need to have the family around. When you are an orphan, there is no one to attend meticulously to these details.

But each day seemed to whiz past faster as my wedding date approached closer, and there seemed to be no time at all to even mull over the changes that would take place while entering a new life, the alterations in personality, the shift in expectations, the changes in behaviour, the complete turnaround in interactions with the change from Miss to Mrs.

3

Paneer Boy Strikes

Love me, love my paneer—was perhaps the most important character trait of my husband. Everything else stemmed from there and was a by-product of or was related to it.

In fact, if you boil a hundred litres of milk, add a dash of home-made vinegar, bring to a boil and then sieve the concoction, you will get an 80-kg Paneer Boy—my soon to be husband. Tall, fair and handsome with a creamy white complexion, would be the best description of the physical characteristics of my husband for an advertisement in the matrimonial columns. He was big-built (he was Punjabi, what did you expect?) and almost six feet tall. He had small, smiling eyes, thin eyebrows and chubby cheeks, like a new born's. Each time he held my hand in his hands, it would be dwarfed by the size of his palms—soft and plump as they were.

So how did I meet Paneer Boy and get married to him?

My wedding was a lovely arranged marriage signed, sealed and delivered by my maternal aunt, the unofficial matriarch of the family who derived unadulterated joy by arranging the marriages of the girls in the extended family. The thrill that I experience losing a few kilograms, she experiences fixing marriages. I think she has singlehandedly masterminded over 5,000 marriages in a span of sixty-five years, being around eighty-four years old currently. She knew my to-be husband's family and had, in fact, attended my prospective in-laws' wedding. She'd effectively known my husband's family socially for about four decades. Sometime around 1996, when I had just lost my mother, my aunt arranged an informal meeting between my soon to be mother-in-law and me at a common friend's house. I knew no details, but my aunt invited me over and since I was quite fond of her and also respected her, I went.

I had just lost my mother, and was too devastated to even think of marriage. I was all alone in the world and felt as though I was a piece of driftwood, floating aimlessly. While my relatives and extended family felt that marriage was the next step for me, the solution to me being all alone in the world, I was just grappling with how to live without Mummy.

As far as I was concerned this meeting was just a 'show your face' meeting without any intention of taking it ahead and with no real marriage agenda, at least from my end. Little did I know that my aunt and soon to be in-laws had been in regular touch for around two years and had been working behind the scenes to arrange a marriage between her elder son and me. You see, my soon-to-be mother-in-law liked me and wanted to make me her daughter-in-law. Around October 1998, my aunt orchestrated the meeting between the families, which essentially was between her (representing my side of the family) and my soon-to-be in-laws. I hadn't met the man I was supposed to marry just yet since he was travelling. I was asked for my photograph for him to see and 'approve' of, a part and procedure of the usual drama of an arranged marriage.

Since I had no parents or any brothers to drop off my photographs, I dropped them off myself on my way back from work at around 8.30 p.m. My prospective father-in-law seemed shocked at this unconventional behaviour and I could sense that I had done something inappropriate—I wasn't sure just what. I came to know much later, when I got married, that my father-in-law felt that this was unorthodox behaviour and disapproved of it. But for once, my father-in-law's observations were disregarded because my soon-to-be husband liked my photograph and 'approved' of me.

So we met a few times, as many times as was permissible within the framework of an arranged marriage, at Khar Gymkhana and various coffee shops, to see whether we were suitable for each other. The conversations were centred on general topics, some personal likes and dislikes and, of course, we both were on our best behaviour, wearing our brightest smiles, smartest clothes, best attitude and putting our best foot forward. So on the surface we seemed to get along—intelligent, well-educated and from good families. And really how much does one find out about what lurks beneath the surface sheen in a few allowed meetings in an arranged marriage? Especially when both families wait in the wings to find out the results of the meeting. Well, both Paneer Boy and I gave pass marks to each other in the examination of arranged marriage setting and conveyed this to the family elders.

It had been two years since my mom had passed away, and I was also beginning to see some logic in what my relatives were saying about marriage, although, I wasn't fully convinced that marriage is the solution to the problem of being alone in the world and the key to the Kingdom of Heaven. After all, on paper I could tick the check boxes of PB's qualities and the match seemed fine. We decided to get married and conveyed this to the family elders because after all, in an arranged marriage, they're the ones that call the shots.

The talks for the marriage started in full swing when there was an unexpected turn of events. My soon to be mother-in-law called up and informed my aunt that her husband was against the marriage and it emerged that it was because he wasn't aware of the actual details of the meetings between Paneer Boy and me. He didn't know that there was a marriage being planned and he hadn't been consulted about this 'marriage proposal' or about the marriage. I, my soon-to-be mother-in-law and husband had unilaterally taken the decision to approve of me and also arrange the marriage and proper protocol of the house hadn't been followed.

My aunt, who could see her dreams of a marriage fixed by her going up in smoke, went into matchmaking overdrive and used up all her relatives, friends and marriage connections to find out the real reason. But despite the father-in-law not giving the go-ahead, PB had really liked me, so he was sticking to his guns about really wanting to marry me. After this my aunt relaxed because now she had an ace up her sleeve. In her words, 'Since the boy is in love, no one can stop him.'

After intense, heated discussions between my soon-to-be husband and my aunt and a few other relatives, all the problems were ironed out and when my father-in-law also agreed to the marriage, our marriage plans resumed. The elders discussed the arrangements of the marriage and well, like I mentioned before, I was involved in everything as I was an orphan.

Soon they went into overdrive and ultimately on 3 December 1998, I made the transition from Miss Shah to Mrs B. The wedding was simple and classy like my wedding card, white with burnished gold detailing, inviting everyone to witness the wedding nuptials and bless the couple.

I wouldn't call my husband fat, but he wasn't lean either. He definitely had brute strength as he was a boxer in school and college. He never wore jeans, only trousers. He was rather formal not only in his dressing but also in his ways of life. He didn't tolerate casualness. Our dressing styles and fashion sense were as similar as the north and south poles.

He always wore formal black or brown well-polished shoes, whereas I was always in flat sandals or if we were going out, I would be in sky-high, vertigo-inducing stilettos.

I spent most of my college life wearing distressed jeans, torn at precarious spots, with a singlet and had permed hair, which I hardly ever combed. In fact, I don't think I even possessed any kind of formal clothes in college. For formal functions, my mother would force me to wear a salwar kameez which I would agree to, provided I could design them. I would get them tailored in 'designer style' and wear culottes instead of the salwar. Unsurprisingly, for my mom, even that was a better choice than the pairs of jeans I loved to wear, ones she considered to be rags. Despite these distinctly different ways of dressing we were quite a good-looking couple.

His thoughts were very conservative, almost Victorian in their quality and severity. He didn't seem to notice the changing world around him and that people were thinking, dressing and living differently. He wanted to embrace a stiflingly regressive way of life. It was like being in a room that hasn't been aired enough and hence has the stale musty smell of mothballs. I was like the wind which was calm but could also become a speedy gale—I was always moving and willing to change. Maybe opposites do attract and that's why we were together.

His attitude towards money can be summed up in one line—I am not my wife's ATM machine. He'd been clear that I wasn't to go around asking him for money any time I fancied something. He maintained that I needed to exercise caution and restraint while asking for money, and definitely while spending it. I called him stingy, he called himself cautious. He was educated and well-spoken, came from a wealthy family and was used to comforts in life but was quite adjusting if the need arose, a sign of good breeding. He wouldn't embarrass anyone thus further emphasizing his good upbringing. I too had these qualities. So we were both brought up as well-rounded individuals—at least it seemed so on the surface.

We were also similar in that we weren't judgemental about others and believed in 'live and let live'. But here one important difference emerged. I would accept a different point of view regardless of the impact it had on me whereas he would only accept it if it didn't contradict his views. If it did, he would try and bring the person to his way of thinking either by convincing or by browbeating them into it. I personally thought this was a waste of time because embracing distinctly different thoughts lead to the growth of an individual.

His only drawback was being afraid to stand by any decisions he made and see them through to the end, even if they were right, for fear of being cut off from the family wealth. Or maybe it was because of a misplaced sense of loyalty to his parents, or perhaps a combination of both. This was especially true in controversial situations which didn't meet the approval of the family. In these situations he would always look for a convenient scapegoat to pin the blame on, as though he was being forced to do something that he didn't want to.

This fixation of always being the 'good guy' and constantly seeking approval especially from his family was his biggest weakness. This led him to ingratiate himself with them at all times, even at the cost of his own happiness and doing the right thing by another person. It's as though his family would always outweigh anyone else on the other side of the scale. His decisions always flip-flopped because, I think, he just didn't have the confidence to stand by them.

Of course, as all Indian sons, he was smothered with love by his mother and was tied, a bit, to her apron strings. I wish mothers in India would let their sons grow up and not burden them with their love. If you love him so much that you can't share him with anyone then don't get him married to anyone else, marry him yourself. But yes, he checked all the right boxes.

- ☑ Good family:
- ☑ Well-known family:
- ☑ Conventionally good looking:
- ☑ Intelligent:
- ☑ Wealthy family:
- ☑ Educated:
- ☑ Employed:
- ☑ A good future:

His name, you ask? Now that is something I won't disclose as some mummies will run to get their daughters married to him after inundating him with sweets and lots of dowry. Perhaps after reading this account, no one would want to get married to him. I don't know which fate is worse—not being married, or being married to him.

4

Fairy Tale Ending or Fairy Tale Ended

Prince meets Princess and they live happily ever after.
Paneer Prince meets Vandy and they live (un)happily ever after.
Fairy tales are enchanting, glamorous, romantic, poetic.
T-H-A-P-A-K

Fairy tales are imaginary, make-believe and mythical.

One T-H-A-P-A-K and reality hit me as I landed on the ground with a hard thud.

Is this what the death of a relationship feels like? I sure felt like a million bucks—overdrawn.

Why is it that when things are good, even nagging feels like love, a prickly beard feels velvety and poverty, romantic? But once things start to skid, it all goes downhill and there comes a point when nothing can make it right. When you start fighting over anything and everything, when these fights never get resolved but add up for another time and escalate into wars, you know your time is up. You start spending more and more time in the office, even more than probably the night watchman, sometimes doing nothing, but staring at the sea. Your boss, at least, starts to appreciate you a bit.

When your husband starts spending more time at the gym and every night out is a boy's night out; when you wish you would not be invited to public functions where your presence would be required as a couple; when you even wish that your mother-in-law comes to visit so that your husband would be busy with her; or when your life together is just a load of bullshit and the mirage of being a couple is just that . . . a mirage, your relationship is in trouble. It's either time to see a counsellor—which is another stigma in Indian society—or it's time to pack up and move on.

The ultimate decay of a relationship is the sum total of a number of incidents that keep adding up until one day, there is irreparable damage. It reaches a stage when you have nothing in common with your husband, the irritation mounts, the unhappiness is all-pervasive, happy moments disappear like the early morning dew on a leaf and soon you can't stand the sight of him. The squabbles become quarrels which then turn into full-blown fights and when you sit back and think, sometimes the reasons are so insignificant that they didn't even merit a mention. But because you are just not meant for each other, you end up attacking each other so mercilessly that you give a new intensity to the phrase 'fighting like cats and dogs'.

According to my husband, I just couldn't do anything right. If I wore jeans, I was fast. If I spoke to a man, I was having an affair with him. If I wanted to get back to my career, I had a hidden agenda of wanting to ignore him and the house (and be with my useless, characterless friends) and to get back to my cheap life, before marriage to him, transformed and uplifted me.

According to him, I wanted to humiliate the family by working in advertising because only whores and characterless women worked in that field. When I couldn't pass my time at home staying idle because having worked most of my adult life I was a better time manager—the housework which was supposed to occupy wives the whole day, I was able to finish in two hours—I was penalized instead of being praised for it. It was as though they thought that I was a loafer who only wanted to waste both their time and money. If this is the state just two months into the marriage, how will you spend a lifetime, or as per Hindu scriptures seven lifetimes, together, they said.

I just didn't understand where all these accusations were coming from and more importantly, the thought process underlying them. Maybe Paneer Boy and I were just two different people. I had never seen behaviour like this while growing up and was really shell-shocked by this belligerence and the baselessness of it all. They were just impractically and impossibly conservative and I was raised as a modern, independent girl.

It was like I was supposed to get cast in an expected and set daughter-in-law mould the instant I got married, without any idea about what this mould was. And Paneer Boy set himself to the husband mode. He had shown me a completely different side of his personality—modern and educated—when we were in the courtship phase. The minute we exchanged garlands, and spent the wedding night together, he showed me the monster within—dark, conservative, weak and living in the dark ages where men were the masters and women just as an accessory. It was quite a Dr Jekyll and Mr Hyde transformation.

I really thought of him as a Double Agent of Love—one personality when we were courting and a completely different one when we were married. Very soon I could see the seams of our marriage straining to split wide open. Or maybe we were just two different people.

I had so many unspoken questions for my in-laws, like, why they didn't get a girl from a less urban background to marry their son. Why bring an educated, Bombay girl into the house? Wasn't I to be given any time to adjust into a new family? Weren't they going to help me to fit into their family? Wasn't I like a daughter to them, as they had proudly proclaimed when we were engaged, because my parents weren't alive? Wasn't the boy supposed to adjust at all? Why was all the adjustment expected to be from the girl's end? Would they constantly judge me by their unspecified, impossible-to-reach standards so that each time I tried to reach the mark of approval, the bar would be set a little higher? If they just wanted an obedient, docile companion why did they not get a dog? I guess it would be difficult to get the dog to cook and have sex with it. But I guess they wanted it all—a good-looking, well-educated, working woman that they could show off to their friends but also someone who essentially didn't have a backbone.

To top it all, there was a lot of interference from my controlling father-in-law. I wouldn't be surprised if he had passed on a manual to Paneer Boy with instructions about how a wife must be kept, about how he must treat his wife like she is a personal slave. I wondered if that manual also had a little side instruction about sex, or was that page left empty because in their world women didn't have needs—it was done for a higher reason like procreation.

My father-in-law would keep a tight rein on the accounts and would tally his accounts every morning, waking up at the unearthly hour of 4 or 5 a.m., before going to the office. And these people were branding me a misfit. But how do you really fit in if your marriage has not had any time to grow? If it is constantly going to be in the shadow of the control and dictates of the in-laws, how will it ever thrive and flourish? For most of the part, I thought of my husband in the collective pronoun 'they', because there were just too many people in my marriage. Instead of just the husband and wife, there was a brigade of in-laws and their advisors. I guess my marriage was as crowded as a suburban train, during rush-hour traffic.

A good and successful marriage needs to have the husband and the wife as the principal players and they should be allowed to settle into it and sort out all the differences that crop up during the teething phase. If this does not happen, the teeth will become poisonous vampire fangs that will draw blood and suck the life out of your marriage, leaving you with the corpse of a relationship instead of a vibrant marriage. With the constant steering and backseat driving, Paneer Boy and I just didn't have the space to grow into each other.

Paneer Boy was a parrot, a spokesperson for my in-laws most of the time. I don't think his parents ever let him develop his own personality, especially at that point in our marriage. If he didn't stand up for himself then, it would never happen. It was his marriage, and his life—they should have just cut the umbilical cord of control.

Even when we were sent to Aurangabad for about three months for office work—we were 'sent' because we really had no say in the matter, it was a family decision and we had to abide by it—there was the constant pressure of being controlled and monitored. For heaven's sake, it's a marriage, not the launching of Apollo 3 into space that we needed constant surveillance.

Once when I was talking to my mother-in-law, she remarked about what had been cooked in my house for lunch the previous day. In Aurangabad. When I asked her how she knew, she unwittingly blurted out how 'every evening my beta calls me up to give me a daily progress report'. So at least their obsession for food and cooking made me aware of their inherent motto—monitor, control. This was not love—this was like a nuchal cord wrapped 360 degrees around a baby's neck which can ultimately kill the infant in the womb. That's the reason doctors cut the umbilical cord, to give the baby its own life. I wish my in-laws had done it and not strangulated Paneer Boy, and me along with him.

It's not what Paneer Boy told his mother that mattered as much as the principle behind it. One day he reported on the food, then the next day it might be something more private and then a minor disagreement becomes a major discord which ultimately contributes to the chopping of your happy marriage into little pieces. It made no sense to me. She didn't need to know everything that was going on in our lives. There was no need for a ball by ball commentary of the daily happenings of her son's married life. I couldn't understand why she couldn't let him be— it was his life and they should have let him build it for himself instead of living vicariously through him.

It is true that my mother-in-law unwittingly and father-in-law knowingly initiated, contributed to and caused the death of my marriage. The irony is that the mehendi applied on my hands during the marriage ceremonies left a dark impression and the myth surrounding it states that if the colour of the mehendi is dark, you will get a lot of love from your in-laws. Looking at the state of my marriage, I knew that this mehendi myth was just that, a myth.

Initially, though I smelt something foul, the smell was faint. Soon it got stronger and finally I had to hold my nose when the stench became unbearable because in the corner of the room I saw the decaying corpse of 'what once was our alive relationship'.

And then T-H-A-P-A-K!

5

T-h-a-p-a-k

Am I imagining it? Am I delusional? The demarcation between imagination and the truth is sometimes just a thin, blurred line, enough to make you doubt your sanity. Your intelligence which may be bordering on genius does nothing to clarify or even darken this line. After all, if you are intelligent this should not be happening to you, isn't it? If you are bright, you should not have to be sitting here, justifying it? If you have even a certain degree of common sense you should be running away as far as possible from this. The blurred line is only in your mind because the imprint on your face, the bruises on your body—that's definitely not the result of a fall, down the stairs. The darkness around your eyes which neither make-up nor lies can conceal is a reality you are too ashamed to admit, for no fault of yours.

After all, aren't you the one at the receiving end?

T-h-a-p-a-k

No, the problem would not go away if you behaved better or didn't defend yourself or gave the right answer. The problem would not disappear if you didn't have so much spirit or were docile and played along. The gravity of the situation wouldn't lessen if only you didn't have tender skin, like your mother's, which bruises easily. Maybe if you cooked like Nigella Lawson,* looked like Aishwarya Rai, and were a corporate hotshot like Indra Nooyi, or a superwoman like Shobhaa Dé, this would not happen.

T-H-AP-A-K

Everything around the 'event' ran through my head, but the actual occurrence. Doesn't half the world (or 80 per cent) live in denial and yet manage perfectly well? Well, so would I. I had studied psychology, and had been the topper in class so I am sure I would excel in denial and sure enough, for a long time I did. After all, it was my fault that the business wasn't doing well and I had most certainly brought only ill luck to their family since the day I got married into the family. It surely had to be my fault that before I got married I had a life and unfortunately, a past, for which I had to suffer and perform a penance. The punishment, of course, could be meted out at any time for any reason but having a past was a good enough reason, more than any other, since a girl's character is the most important thing, at least in India.

---

* By the time the book goes to print it was out in the public space that even she was being physically abused.

What really defines character? Being honest, paying your taxes, having saved yourself for your husband? Character is such a difficult concept to describe and yet so many women are subjected to immense ostracism due to this superfluous description. In India by saying *'Character kharab hain'*—she is of a bad character—about a person always gives you the moral right and superiority to behave the you want with that person.

T-h-a-p-a-k t-h-a-p-a-k

I kept telling myself that I must have done something to anger my husband. I would tell myself that I shouldn't burden him with my problems. I reasoned that it was but natural that he was tired after being at work all day and if I talk to him about problems at home, and he behaves like this, he is surely only reacting to fatigue. He was always so loving, I told myself, he must be having a bad day to react like this. It was my fault. I was the stupid one for not understanding what he really wanted—I must improve and be more patient.

My arguments always ended with 'I must improve' and with this pledge I would continue to live with him another day and love him another day. It isn't difficult to love anyone in a situation when you feel that you are unworthy of their love and keep struggling to become worthy of it. I also struggled with my belief that my fairy-tale marriage must continue not only for my sake but also for the sake of society. I became a champ at evading the main issue. After all, it was my fault one way or the other. 'I must improve' was my mantra. Every day I would think that this mantra would change my life. It did but not in quite the way I imagined it.

When the marks became too obvious my make-up became stronger. I used dark eye shadow even in the mornings, deep pink rouge, red lipstick and enough pancake to put Bollywood to shame. In fact, I used to muse to myself that MAC would make a killing if they targeted this audience—the abused wives' club membership growing by the second. I started thinking of newer excuses to make to acquaintances, to social friends, and even to my closest friends. Some of my stories began to sound like fairy tales to my own ears, or worse still, like the old Ramsay horror flicks—patchy, vulgar and implausible. But I just didn't think of the main issue.

T-h-a-p-a-k T-h-a-p-a-k T-h-a-p-a-k

There was no point telling anyone about what was going on either. After spending endless days and nights dissecting the pros and cons of my circumstances, I was still in a quandary about the way ahead. With courage in my heart but still filled with trepidation, I told a common family friend to help me sort the situation. The response I got was unbelievable. He refused to believe me and said, 'I don't think this is possible. I have known him and the family since he was a school-going boy and he would not do something like this. You must be mistaken.' I pointed to my horrifyingly dark make-up which, by this point, had stopped concealing much. He casually remarked that the marks were nothing and merely shrugged.

His wife was even worse. She said in a hushed tone, 'These things happen, don't take them to heart. When you are young, you have no control over your impulses and you know how men are. With age, he will mellow and then you won't have to worry so much. Keep out of his way for a while and just go with the flow.' But . . . but . . . but . . .' I said, and before I could complete the sentence she raised her hand in the air, to indicate that I wasn't to speak any more, at which point I involuntarily shrank back and receded twenty steps.

She didn't notice my strange behaviour or chose to ignore it and continued with her all-knowing advice. 'You must have a child and then everything will be fine.' I stood rooted in disbelief at this solution. 'Even Mrs Khanna's daughter-in-law was in the same predicament and the minute the child came along, everything was fine. Now I don't think it happens.' Wow, I thought, she is trying to console me by telling me someone else went through the same thing? What were we comparing notes on? Buying the latest Jimmy Choos?

Another thing struck me, she thought that Mrs Khanna's daughter-in-law's problem had abated, but she wasn't sure. Outwardly, I nodded absent-mindedly.

Inside, there was a storm brewing at the injustice of it all combined with the apathy of the people around me. No one wanted to acknowledge that a problem existed. They spent hours and days and maybe even a lifetime denying it. It was like having AIDS. For if you are an AIDS patient, everyone thinks that you are at fault and it's the guilt of it that kills you almost as much as the disease. When they do acknowledge its existence, you are held responsible for bringing it upon yourself. You are shamed into guilt and mentally beaten into submission because it is, after all, your fault.

The instamagic cure to the problem is like the fountain of youth—it doesn't exist. The antidotes range from simplistic and foolish remedies like that universal cure for all diseases in married couples' lives—having kids—to never ever acknowledging the truth, to absolutely derecognizing your individuality. Everything is on offer but the truth.

So you are really between a rock and a hard place. Neither is your problem acknowledged and since it doesn't exist, there is no solution. The frustration of physical hurt coupled with the greater aggravation of not being believed and being stigmatized as a traitor if you speak up are probably the reasons no one has been able to really put an end to domestic abuse. So the vicious cycle continues where the aggressor is feted and the victim is reviled.

Why is this experience the most painful to speak about, even more than poverty? It's only when I started speaking about this and did so in the third person (I sometimes still do) did I realize that it was acute and chronic. I also wrote about it in the third person and said that it had happened to a friend of mine. But the truth is, it was happening to me.

I am not a victim, and rarely portray myself as one. I don't look the part and I don't have that mental frame, yet this definitely made me feel victimized. I felt helpless like a rat trapped in a maze of mirrors with no way out. For the longest of time, I just blamed myself for everything.

I never even acknowledged that it happened. So many questions came to my mind at that time when the violence was going on and the biggest of them was 'why me?' That was also the time I remembered God and my mum the most as she not only loved me but was also a brave no-nonsense woman and of course my Dad the fearless fighter pilot who fought three wars—they would have been horrified to see me become this weakling getting clobbered by a brute. I really wished that this triumvirate would save me if not by coming to my help physically then at least in spirit and give me the courage and strength to stand up for myself. I wished that I was brave, had someone to support me—an angel to give me a guiding hand.

I would think that I had been quite a good person till now. I had looked after my mother so many times when she was hospitalized because of her cancer—this happening to me just did not add up. Maybe the Universe meant it for someone else and this was happening to me by mistake. I just couldn't see any real and fathomable reason for all this to be happening to me. I wish I was more my parents' daughter and stood up for myself. I wish, I wish, I wish . . .

Oh yes, I forgot to tell you what was happening to me, or was I trying to evade the real issue yet again?

I was getting beaten . . . by my spouse.

★★★

When a bird is caged and is not tame enough to stay in the cage, what do you do? Of course, at first you try and withdraw food, then water, then you shout at it, and then some more, and then finally you cut its wings to prevent it from fighting and leave it to die. When it still doesn't die, in frustration you hold it by its neck and even throw it out of the cage because you want the cage empty. When the cage is empty you just go ahead and get another bird.

Before you get another bird, you eliminate all traces of the first bird and polish the cage to make it look brand new. Then what happens to the almost-dead bird with broken wings? Who cares? She is not your concern. You are a getting a new bird. The bird story is the story of my life.

Can I be a hypocrite and say that I was unhappy from day one? No. The marriage was not bad from Day One. It was okay. But things can get better, I reasoned. My eternal optimism and the fact that every marriage takes time to blossom kept me going. To my mind, each day is a fresh day and there are no negative carry forwards from the previous day. You cannot remember every slight or curse or harsh word because life is too short and you have to move forward.

But he had an elephant's memory which he used to great effect to remind me that it was all my fault. He said repeatedly that my parents had taught me nothing and since they were dead, where would I go? My faults were numerous. I laughed too loudly; I listened to music; I liked thanking God for all that I had; I wanted to work; I had friends; I had a life before I got married; I used to talk to people; I used to talk to strangers and ask for help; I went to a college that encouraged loose-charactered people; I made bad food because my mother had taught me nothing; there were so many other girls who would have given their life to be as lucky as I was; I didn't want to do what was considered decent things; I was too posh; I was a fraud, a fake; I had conned him into marrying me; I was a liar, a loser; I had no one to support me; I must have also caused my parents to die; I should not even make eye contact with the driver because that means I want to sleep with him; I worked in advertising.

Till I was disciplined enough to learn the ways of their family I should not have a child I was told. After all, if I did, how would I raise a kid—I was so useless, I could not even look after myself. How could I be trusted to bring another person into this world?

I just wasn't upto the mark.

So I must have physical marks on my body and emotional marks in my psyche as constant reminders to upgrade myself. My husband took this job upon himself because, of course, he was from a cultured family and they always knew best. Any resistance just meant that you had to be put down—not bent, but completely broken.

Now I know why he won the boxing championships in his college. He was really good. I got free boxing lessons and learnt things like if your opponent lets down his guard even for a minute you could have a stranglehold on his neck and bring him down on the mat and then the next round starts. He could punch, sock, use the upper cut on the jaw and could even twist your arm before you knew it. Maybe he was missing his college days and I was the latest punching bag in town. He was a true champion and I was, well you already know what—I was A NOTHING.

The key element in boxing is surprise. In my case, it was

not surprise, but absolute shock at being treated like this one day and then the next day having to pretend it hadn't happened and even chat about inane things like, 'We should get the car mats cleaned by a professional cleaner, this guy who washes our car every day is really not that good'. I would cry at the hypocrisy of it all, not at my marks but at the absolute degradation of being a non-person.

Each time this would happen, I would swear to myself that this was the last time I had taken this from him. When the physical pain would be unbearable and the bruises would turn dark, I would touch them delicately, nurse them and promise myself that this was the last time this would happen. But then would come the patch-up phase where he would be so endearing. He would buy me flowers, apologize profusely, take me out for dinner, promise that we would be the happiest couple in the world, talk about having children and how I was the best wife one could ask for. We would chat, make love, maybe go out for a movie and I would soon forget everything, thinking that it was a one-off, a temporary phase and all was well.

Nothing like this would ever happen again.

But then the abuse would start unexpectedly, where for no fault of mine, I would be corrected in the way that he thought best. Once when I was crying and clutching at his leg through his trouser, feeling the material in my hands, all the while sitting on the floor begging him not to leave me, I wondered about how and when I had become so fearful, helpless, weak, dependent and depressed. I wondered what had happened to the brave, strong, intelligent, fun-loving girl who got married to this man. That girl seemed like a mirage and 100 million miles away from this one in her place.

I hated myself for having become this but every time I would promise myself that this was the last time I was going to put up with this torture, my resolve would just dissolve. I was just not myself. I had become a completely different person who had no self-respect or any faith in herself. The fear of public knowledge of the failure of a marriage and the ostracism that follows makes you want to keep believing that everything will work out.

After all, quite often in India, once you are married you are the property of the husband and he can do what he likes—use, abuse, throw, and repeat the cycle ad infinitum. No one comes to intervene because it is between you and your husband. Anyone who comes in between is a third person and really has no right to speak as it is a private matter and must be sorted out by the husband and wife. When you speak out, it is time to cut you off because you know nothing and are nobody. You are invisible.

Do you just bring your family's name in the mud and go to the cops and make a complaint? 'Decent people' just don't do that. Do you scream out and ask for the neighbours to help. No, because then they'll find out what is going on. Do you just run away from the house? But where will you go; ultimately you will have to come back here. So you just keep playing this cat and mouse game and then actually thank God for the days that you can walk around without the dark eye make-up and have your natural look.

Till one day even that is not acceptable and you are

dragged by your hair, held against the wall and just pushed, pushed, pushed out of the house, and asked threateningly never ever to come back or in which case the cops will be called because it was his father's property and I was an intruder there.

I can't even remember the reason why I was physically pushed out of their home after midnight. It's ironic because it was they who had repeatedly drilled into me that I should never be out alone at this time, as only characterless girls are out at night. It was something really minor that escalated into mayhem. They pushed me out of the door and slammed it shut in my face whilst I stood there with tears streaming down my cheeks. I stood outside for a long time and kept begging them to let me back into the house. Then I started banging on the door. For some time I just sat outside on the floor with my head resting on my knees crying by myself. When all my cries fell on deaf ears I slowly started walking down the stairs all the while crying and mumbling to myself like a deranged person. Because I was deranged by grief. I briefly stood near the parking lot in the building and looked up and shouted out to them to let me in. But their windows along with their hearts were shut to me. I knew that the only door and heart that would always remain open to me would be my mother's house, my *maika*.

The mindset of an abused woman is that of a bird with broken wings—defeated, senseless and the very thing that will release her—wings—she has none. It takes a lot of healing and courage to learn to fly again. Somewhere along the way your love becomes laced with fear and your aggressor is the very person you turn to, to be your protector. A completely self-destructive cycle. Even someone like me could not break free of it till I was actually forced to break free of it. Your wings are cut and you limp off back to your nest but you do make it because at least you are alive.

6

He-Divorces-Me . . .
He-Divorces-Me-Not . . .

As a teenager I used to play the 'he-loves-me, he-loves-me-not' game with more daisies than I can even count. The 'he' usually was my crush of the week and the final petal decided the fate of our love life. Today I was doing the same thing except that the chants accompanying the petals were 'he-divorces-me, he-divorces-me-not' and it was no longer a harmless adolescent game but a deadly adult one.

I don't remember how I got to my mom's house after they threw me out. I sat outside on the steps because I didn't have the house keys. Then I walked up to Bobby's house, the lady who used to work at our home. She lived barely 200 metres from my mum's house, so I trudged to her house in the night, dragging my feet heavily with a blank mind. As I stood outside her tiny one-room tenement in a slum and called out her name, it struck me how alone I was. She came out looking drowsy and said in a matter-of-fact voice, without any shock or surprise, 'You have come back.'

As I nodded, she said, 'Didi but now I don't have the keys of the house. You took all the keys with you.' I just kept mum, because I was too numb to even speak. Bobby just took over and said, 'OK let's go to the house.'

I just followed her like a child following her mother, full of trust and confidence, that the mother will know what to do. We went back to the house and sat down on the steps on the landing outside the flat. We didn't converse, there was no need to. It is true that sometimes silence is the best conversation. After a couple of hours she said, 'Let's go and have tea.'

It was understood that we would go to her house because my house was still locked as I didn't have the key. Even then I understood the ironic reality of the situation, all alone in this world with all the people who are related to me by blood who are supposed to help, but will never be there except to run me down and all I had was a relative stranger, a hired house help, who is so poor but has the heart of a king. It formed the basis of my beliefs that not birth but actions and love create and sustain relationships.

We went to her house and had the sickeningly sweet tea that she used to make and then after I refused to eat anything, we trudged back to my house. She remarked, 'I have the key maker's number and I can call him up at 6.30 or 7 in the morning.'

At about 6.30 in the morning she called him up and

when he came and saw me his only remark, which made me crack into the first smile and welcomed me into my new life, was, 'Didi, you have lost the keys . . . again. Anyways, no problem. I'll make a new set.' So this new set of keys reopened the door to my new Forcefully Born Again Single Married life.

A few months had passed since I had been kicked out of the golden cage and surprisingly, one day, out of the blue, I got a phone call from Paneer Boy saying that he wanted to meet me. I forced myself not to attach any great weightage to this phone call. I did not want to overthink the reason for the call. But it was impossible not to think about its significance and what it meant for our future. After hours of deliberation and exhaustive, non-productive, circuitous thinking I went to meet him expecting the best and also expecting nothing.

I got dressed to the nines and took an auto to go and meet him at a hotel in Juhu, where he said he wanted to meet. After we finished ordering coffee, he came straight to the point and said he came to meet me to tell me that it was over and they had decided to divorce me. Even here he referred to our marriage and divorce as a collective decision rather than an individual one. The minute he told me I started sobbing my guts out. As he started consoling me, we started talking and discussing our lives. Since we had started living separately, we both realized we were unhappy without each other. After talking for two hours we realized that our marriage had major teething problems and too much interference from 'others'. We also decided that we would change our respective behaviours and I made it clear that any kind of physical and mental violence wouldn't be tolerated. The more we spoke the more convinced we became that there was still enough juice left in the marriage. We decided to give it another shot.

Violence and domestic abuse were non-negotiable.

After he settled the cheque there was no more hemming and hawing. We had come separately, he in his car and me in an auto, and we directly went back to my home and made out like two lustful teenagers. We came there as two individuals and left as a couple.

The funny and exciting part is that our courtship started during those days after we were already married. He would come to my home after work and not inform anyone that he was coming to see me. We'd make love, he would eat a little, replenishing his body after hard work, then he'd head off home to his parents, who were, of course, clueless about this arrangement. I thought our lovemaking would give us away—the musty fragrance and the sexy demeanour. I guess all that my in-laws had done for so long was count money and they knew nothing about any of these pleasures.

The romantic experiences that one has before marriage seemed to have started after my marriage—surreptitious meetings, hidden romance, wanton lust. It had all the ingredients of a romantic novel with a twist where our romance was conducted as a cloak and dagger affair between a lawfully wedded husband and wife. We had to act like undercover agents of love because as per the wishes of his family, we were to be divorced not engaging in this romantic saga. Because I wanted this marriage to work so desperately, I agreed to hide our renewed relationship from the world.

I'd give him blank calls on the home phone and he'd know it was me and then come and call from the grocer's. Cell phone calls back then cost Rs 32 a minute so we would used them sparingly and I had to consider my money or rather the lack of it. We would whisper sweet nothings into the phone. And, of course, the grocer, who was at Pali Hill near my husband's home, thought my husband was having an affair till he met me and I told him that it was me he was calling, the legitimate Indian wife.

In India, we seem to have this inherent need to justify our actions to everyone even if they aren't a part of our family and of course we must at every stage come across as very good. We also love our spouses in a strange, constant, chronic way like I did, and are willing to put up with them despite all odds, like I did with my husband. I ended up sometimes comparing him to my ex-boyfriend and I knew my husband didn't really match up. Quite often, although it is not an openly acknowledged fact, sometimes even to ourselves, women think of their ex-boyfriends or crushes or crushed romances. While with their husbands, and even otherwise, at times something will unsheathe an old memory.

And so, we enjoyed being with each other, his sweet, fair, chubby face kissed me like an amateur, but a man in love; his tall, big body held me close; and he had the strangest aroma of body heat, mixed with innocence, some Hugo Boss and Cinthol soap. He felt good against my thin curvaceous body. All that lovemaking also definitely helped us to bond and I felt we were on our second honeymoon in my small cosy home in Bandra which could have been anywhere in the world. We were a young, good-looking, intelligent city couple in love.

My home was a girl's home and my drawing room which was not really the place for anything but conversations, was great, with a panelling of white and had paintings of flowers hung on it and looked bright and chirpy and inviting like me. The kitchen was modern and was the place where his replenishing food was cooked, right from vada pav to dabeli to Bombay club sandwiches, roadside-style, all made by the efficient house help. The bedroom was cute, flowery and pink, the perfect setting for our impassioned lovemaking. It had a nice double bed, glass windows and of course an AC which ensured we were all set. The inside room was my writing room, tomato red and violet.

At that point, my home was in a state of disrepair due to irregular maintenance. It was a bit like our marriage/ relationship and was perfect for the setting even though I had planned none of this. Oh yes! I always had music playing at home as it kept me pepped up and even though I had no idea that I would end up writing, the music, the fragrance and a little differently done up home kept me creative, at least in my dressing and the jewellery that I wore, all designed by me. So life was good.

Despite my husband and I being voracious readers and great conversationalists, no conversation happened when we were with each other. Since we had such little time together we put it to other use. What would you want two twenty-seven-year-olds to do? It was amazing.

We did plan vacations together and thought of London and France. But we didn't want to spend money at this stage. True, we had no commitments and having a child was nowhere on our agenda, but we wanted to stabilize our marriage so we just spent all the time together and when it was time for him to go home usually at 8 p.m., we were both sad. I was always a little more upset because I would be all alone again.

So our surreptitious meetings continued at my home, that my mum had left me, for three months making the marriage dashing and mysterious. My home had officially become a love/lust nest with its background music and efficient house help, Bobby. Interestingly, Bobby was so named because she ran away with her current husband after watching the movie *Bobby* and refused to answer to any other name. Perhaps it was destined that she would come and work in this nest of mine. Bobby really reinforced my faith in humanity and her shrill, gravelly voice sounded like the voice of hope and life itself. The love, affection, care and understanding she gave me elevated her status to a surrogate mother in my eyes.

During all this time, I remember nothing of my in-laws' house in Pali Hill—repression at best. All I remember is that it never smelled fresh, was stuffy, cramped my style and that I never liked the food. I used to sneak out and eat burgers and chips at this joint called Candies, and then go home and tell my mother-in-law that I was dieting and eat only fruit.

But you can't keep life at bay forever. Our lovemaking and our madness of being in love, and a dream chance of a second shot at marriage would have continued till eternity and kingdom come till in stepped a relative who as everyone knows is always a bearer of bad news. One of my aunts decided to come home unannounced that day to give me another lecture about my bad behaviour and discuss my bad karma and hence my suffering of being alone. She was getting all comfortable and strident in her preachy avatar when out sprang my husband from my bedroom and informed her that all was well in the marriage. She was left open-mouthed and immediately changed her stance to talk about my good behaviour, accumulation of my good karma and other such platitudes.

She started calling up and collected a gang of relatives and went to meet his parents to inform them of the mating and meeting. They had heard rumours of the impending divorce and relatives being relatives decided to go to my in-laws' home to prove to my in-laws that they were wrong and that their son had been meeting me and that the divorce talks should be quashed. My in-laws refused to believe it and started demanding back the jewellery they had given me and insisting I sign the divorce papers.

But my husband never spoke up, again displaying his weak character and maybe his susceptibility to emotional blackmail. There were enough hysterics to top a Rajshri production or an Amy Winehouse song and maybe a Jen Aniston romcom rolled into one. Then after a day he confessed to his parents that he'd been seeing me and that he'd like to live with me.

'All hell broke loose' doesn't even begin to describe what happened. His mum wanted to commit suicide, his father threatened to have a heart attack! How can you decide to have a heart attack? But my father-in-law was a control freak and so willing a heart attack was a minor matter for him! He also threatened to cut Paneer Boy off from the family wealth which would've caused him to have an attack. Paneer Boy's brother accused him of spoiling the family's name and then some more hysterics followed. But for once, he stood his ground to whatever level he could and said he wanted me.

So his dad had to cancel the divorce papers and came to his senses for a while. Then he came to see me at my home to understand my intentions. I couldn't understand why he wanted to talk about this. I was screwed both literally and figuratively. I just wanted to be with my husband and restart life, preferably go to London and just live like a normal married couple, far from the madness and interference of his family.

My father-in-law then came back the next day to my home with an affidavit and he wanted me to sign the documents apologizing to their family on stamp paper. Can you blame me for the state of the relationship and the state of my husband's heart and mind? I was shocked beyond belief and I thought it was a bad joke but the old man was serious. I agreed to sign.

But was he satisfied? He promptly took out another affidavit which claimed that I had taken away all my belongings from their home. This was a lie as I had been kicked out of the house with just the clothes on my back. This document also proclaimed that I would never ever claim their property. This made me finally realize that he is Prem Cheapda, a combination of a villain and a cheapskate. I knew that I was up against so much that only God, karma and destiny could save me. It's not like I had a choice. So, out of a helplessness, which was unlike my nature, without further ado, but still saying a little prayer, I signed it and said, 'Now are you convinced that I love my husband and not his money.'

He just made some remark which I don't remember and then came the whopper. 'He will be staying here with you and we would like that as there is no place in the house till things settle down. You can't even enter that building.' I said bravely: 'Why can't we stay in your other place?' No response. I later found out that they thought I would grab that property or become a squatter there. So again I relented without a fight. What a pushover I had become. I was never like this but I guess when you are put down for a while you lose everything you have and only a Herculean effort can save you.

So where was my brave husband during all this? He had disappeared, apparently on work, and was of course out of town. He was a coward but I did love him and had to choose between the devil and the deep blue sea. I chose him over the property and staying alone. And I did love my husband. I just didn't have the courage to end my marriage as I came from a family where my parents were dead and I wished my relatives were too, didn't have too much money, almost a non-existent career and a lot of pride in making a marriage work, come hail or storm.

After this entire brouhaha calmed down, we settled down in my home to rebuild our life together as a couple. I was confident that things had stabilized. I had got a ticket again to the merry-go-round of marriage. I was beginning to enjoy the spinning and could feel the whoosh of the wind in my hair and could smell the sweet taste of success in the marriage that I had heard about from my cousins, aunts, who had extolled the virtues of this institution while convincing me to get married. In my dreams I started celebrating the togetherness, and was almost rejoicing our long, happily married lives with two children when I was jolted out of my reverie. The ironic part then was that even in my dreams I could not see the dream from end to end. Maybe my subconscious was telling me something that my conscious mind wasn't accepting.

But a leopard never changes its spots. The old patterns soon re-emerged and a minor incident escalated into a full blown fight and into yet again another misstep. We had boarded the merry-go-round again and soon we were spinning out of control. I realized then that somewhere my husband's hand had slipped out of mine and I was alone on this . . . MARRY-GO-ROUND. I looked desperately

for him and as I called out to him, I could hear the echo
of my own voice calling back to me, like I was underwater.
When I turned and looked back I could see my husband
in the distance with a bunch of people, some of whom
seemed familiar, some were strangers. I felt breathless, alone
and gasping for air like I was being strangled. Then I could
see a paper coming straight for me. And as I stared at the
alphabets on the paper, I knew for sure I was all alone.

7

Divorce and American Independence Day

Knock, knock.
Who's there?
A sordid divorce petition and my heart stopped.

Despite our steamy patch-up and the papers that I'd signed, waiving off any right to my husband's money, to prove my bona fide intentions to my father-in-law that I genuinely loved my husband and not his money, my husband didn't let me know that he was still planning to get rid of me. I heard some random rumours from equally random relatives. I didn't believe them—my head was telling me to believe them but my heart just didn't want to. I thought he spent all those months with me loving me, taking me out and then loving me more, ensconcing

me in his big brawny body, surely, he'd at least be decent
with me. But I guess the white snake with spectacled
beady eyes—my father-in-law—Mr Prem Cheapda,
didn't want to risk it and just decided to move in directly
for the kill, like a King Cobra. This is because last time my
husband had come to tell me, we had moved in together;
so I guess this time the snake wasn't risking his precious
investment, never mind what my husband wanted, as in
most rich industrialist families the only want, need, desire,
ever taken into consideration is MONEY, MOOOLAH,
CASH in any language or format.

So here I was standing by myself at 9 a.m. in the
morning in my doorway with the door ajar, just staring
uncomprehendingly at the postman, wondering who could
have sent me a letter because most of us friends just emailed
or called each other. I got my answer less than 30 seconds
later when he said in Marathi, 'Something has come from
the court.' I said, 'I don't want it, it's not for me.' He said,
'Are you Bandana Shah?' (That was his way of pronouncing
my name.) I said, in a hysterical, panicky voice, 'Ya, but
this is not for me because this can't be happening to me.' I
didn't feel like me so the postman said, 'Are you taking it or
not?' I said, 'NO! NO! NO!' and he walked away wanting
no part of my drama. Poor guy, after all he was just the
messenger and although you don't shoot the messenger of
bad news, I was forcibly involving him in my life.

So what did I do? I sobbed for a bit and then called my
friend, Sunil Doshi, in Bandra. He lived in a fancy house
and his dad was a Padmashree so I thought he'll know

what to do. Damn, the phone wasn't working, so I went to call from a local phone, still wearing my night suit—cut off black tracks and a tank top with no bra. I just didn't care; clothes and how I looked was the last thing on my mind when my world was slowly but surely crashing. I still decided I would keep a positive outlook and would fight this to the end. Well, my friend turned up at my gate. He was playing table tennis, when I had interrupted his game, at Khar Gymkhana Club. We headed off to the post office, which was less than a kilometre away from my house, in a dangerously driven black and yellow autorickshaw. We reached in less than 5 minutes.

Doshi—skinny as a beanpole thanks to genes, regular playing and walking, walked out of the post office with the petition and decided to put it in the TT bag, which was actually a lawn tennis bag, because he was too stingy to buy a proper bag and this one was about fifty years old and was a gift, and out came tumbling an empty bottle of McDowell whisky and I thought, well I'm asking for guidance and help from this person and then I burst out laughing, saying aloud, 'It can't get any worse than this, so bring it on. I am at the bottom of the pit which is filled with McDowell whisky and from here I can only go higher.'

So we headed off to another club, this one in Santa Cruz—the Willingdon Catholic Gymkhana patronized by the Catholics. Nice place, simple, inexpensive and low key and just what the doctor prescribed at this time. I was an associate member of both these clubs but the two were as different as chalk and cheese. The former was loud and had

so-called businessmen and the latter was frequented mostly
by Catholics who weren't businessmen but service people.

We ordered tea and toast and extricated the petition
from the bag which still had the empty bottle of whisky. I
tell you, why are all my friends crazy like me! The petition
was fifteen pages long and as far as I thought it looked like
junk and suddenly I wasn't scared any more. Anyway, I had
decided to remain optimistic, and brave, even if it meant
faking it.

We ordered for a couple of more strong teas to keep
us going and we read the petition sitting next to the lawn
tennis court as I felt so stifled with the reality of my life
that I could not think of sitting inside. It was around 10
a.m. and since it was the tail end of holidays there were
still quite a few people around. We started reading each
paragraph and the first few just stated facts like we were
married in so and so place on so and so date as per Hindu
rites, we had no kids, our lawyers were so and so.

Then came the salacious juicy parts, dripping with sex.
It said that I was a loose-charactered woman who had
innumerable boyfriends and was not fit to be a wife. It listed
out a few of them and then some. The petition painted me
out to be a whore and stated that I was promiscuous and had
multiple relationships with other men during the course
of our marriage. It made absolutely no sense. It made me
wonder where the time or the energy for these affairs was
since I was newly married and was trying to learn how to
set up home. I had two domestic helps, an elderly woman
and her daughter-in-law, who used to be with me at home

till my husband came back from the office. So where and when was I meeting these men? Unless I was invisible and the domestic helps couldn't see me and it was logistically impossible to meet all of them unless I accommodated them in fifteen-minute slots spread over ten hours?

It was unbelievable. They got the name of my ex-boyfriend from college right so there was at least some truth to it. But what was his relevance here? They also mentioned a girl, Anupam, who had a boy's name, as one of my boyfriends—so much for misplaced enthusiasm. At least their detective who was following me could have got the gender right. For good measure, they even added some of my classmates' names to the petition. The poor guys, I pitied my classmates who were just being dragged into someone else's marital hell for no reason.

The final nail in the coffin of my character assassination was an 'etc. and etc.' at the already exhaustive list of men who I was sleeping with whilst I was married to my husband, as per the petition. Just so more names could be added to the list of men who I was sleeping with. I couldn't believe their nerve at adding an *etc*. If I had all these millions of boyfriends then why did my husband marry me? Considering their paranoid nature, you think they wouldn't have checked up on my background before taking me in as their daughter-in-law?

The next para spoke about my incessant partying, drinking and 'gay lifestyle'. Didn't they accuse me of sleeping with the entire male population and now they are accusing me of being gay—guys, make up your mind,

either I am gay or I am a slut. Which again led to basic
questions like, if I was staying with my husband wouldn't
he have been partying with me, too? It's okay for him to
party but if I do the same I become a loose-charactered
woman. So what's right for the goose is not right for the
gander.

As for drinking, for the record, I do not drink—not
even a teeny tiny drop of wine, no cocktails, no Breezers,
and no lady drinks. All I was thinking was, 'Get real and
don't make a mockery of everything and assume that just
because you are wealthy you can say anything and everyone
will believe it, however ridiculous it sounds. Maybe your
paid flunkies do, so you are used to getting your own way.'

The next para spoke about how much jewellery and
cash they had given me which again was a load of bull.
Whatever little they gave me I went and sold it to a
pawn shop. What was the use of the mangal sutra if the
person for whom you are wearing it is destroying you?
So the exaggeration of these exquisitely carved sets and a
beautiful engagement ring given to me made it laughable. I
thought to myself, 'Hey I have admitted to an ex-boyfriend
who dumped me, to physical and mental abuse from my
husband and to going back for more, in short, to being a
complete loser and having absolutely no faith in myself. So
why on earth would I lie about some jewellery?'

The fairy tale in the petition continued with the next
statement. I had huge property and was worth crores (I
wish). The property of course was in Himachal Pradesh
and could be converted to a resort, so said the petition and

I thought, 'So why don't they buy it and set me free?' In reality this was just barren land which was worthless. Wow! I could look after myself as I was educated and capable and had held a job prior to getting married. If I was so capable, why did always tell me that I was foolish and no good and why did he leave me. If I looked at the bright side, this petition was making me feel great—rich and talented, wow. It's ironic that it took a divorce petition to make them realize my worth.

The next few paragraphs spoke about my bad behaviour like fighting with people on the streets (somewhat true), abusing people, while fighting with them (hmmm true), but who doesn't do that? Of course, the petition conveniently left out that I was fighting to defend a teenage girl, in Aurangabad, who was being eve-teased by a bunch of rowdy cyclists who insisted on talking to her breasts since according to them she had made the mistake of wearing jeans and a T-shirt.

I gave it to those guys with threats and the choicest abuses and they apologized to her and told me, 'Aunty! We won't do it again.' It seemed ridiculous that a boy not five years my junior was now calling me Aunty! The incident was firmly etched in my mind because of two reasons— my husband's hesitation in helping anyone who he didn't perceive directly connected with him, a sort of attitude that reflects that these things happen to and impact others and not us. The second reason, his comment, 'If she had worn a salwar kameez, instead of jeans, this would not have happened to her.' I just stared at him and remember thinking, 'He is supposed to be a modern young man of the 21st century living in one of the poshest localities in the world and he's talking like he just stepped out of the pre-Independence era, Victorian age.' I expressed my views to him, quite vociferously, but he stuck to his point of view and since it seemed like a pointless argument which could escalate into a fight I let it drop. I can't believe it they had included this incomplete distorted version in the petition. What proved their paranoia is that they had affidavits to that effect. I'm sure the affidavits would eventually be of their employees in the office and would not stand up in a court of law.

The petition also said that I had misbehaved and had been suspended from Khar Gymkhana (true) but of course it didn't say it was because at that time the President was my father-in-law's closest friend and was ruling the club like it was his personal fiefdom. They accused me of tearing up a piece of writing paper in the library, claiming that it made a noise and I had violated the rule of 'Keep Silence' in the library, later they changed this to stealing a piece of paper from the library. Let me tell you something. I read about three books a week and in complete silence with music in the background and as all readers know, for us the library is the sanctum sanctorum and we'll never do anything to defile it and why on earth would I create a noise in the library and also steal a piece of paper when there are plenty available for the asking. But, that was the cover story given for suspending me. They tried to expel me, but for that they would have to cancel the membership of my husband since he was a primary member, so the President suspended me, and thereby reinforced his close friendship with my father-in-law, as in true Bollywood-style villains. Currently I was a committee member, and was a fair distance from being either suspended or rusticated.

The last few paras were boring and just said about the relief they sought. They wanted a separation on grounds of cruelty again using an ETC. They had no firm ground for divorce on adultery. Did they think they would get a divorce from me on these grounds? I didn't think it was likely.

The interesting part is that this was drafted by a property lawyer who was one of my father-in-law's retainers. Of course, I would have no claim on property as they had got the affidavit signed by me earlier. In all fairness, the petition didn't have as many spelling errors as other lawyers' works and that probably was the best part. I then reread the entire petition. I just didn't know what to make of it but I could feel a sense of panic rising within me, helplessness that you feel when you can't turn back the clock.

I just stared into nothingness and had flashbacks of my marriage . . . how beautiful I looked; our honeymoon; the fights; the crying; the make-up sex; the plans for the future; the eating out at restaurants; sex; the dolling up to go out; the love bites; the arguments; the vicious fights; the abuses; the cowering in a corner by myself; the pleadings of not to leave me; the crying; the promises of love; the feeling of suffocation; the guilt; fear; dependence; the begging not to leave me; the willingness to do anything to make the marriage work; desire to change to make everything okay; all the fault being mine. Crying, with the tears streaming down my cheeks, in an act of false bravado, I tried to wash away my tears.

My reverie was a jumble of thoughts and yet it gave me a sense of what I had and what I didn't.

For a moment I became pragmatic and tried to approach it in a matter-of-fact manner and took out a pencil and underlined the sections where I felt they were attacking me. After doing this for about twenty minutes, I realized I had underlined the original petition.

How devastated was I that I underlined the original petition? You can imagine the state of my mind where it didn't strike me that I have underlined an original petition. My mind was garbled, like crossed wires broadcasting mangled, distorted images.

I was desperate and myriad thoughts were running in my mind—where, what, when, why, how and the underlying thought, 'Now what do I do.' I was grappling for answers and none were forthcoming. It was like me appearing for multiple exams and failing in all. I felt like I was standing with my hands tied behind me and was being hit by multiple stones and spears. I was unable to defend myself and was eventually collapsing to the ground in a helpless heap. A sense of failure pervaded me and my being. I thought to myself, 'I need to pray hard and this too shall pass.' Then I did pray, in fact I went to the Chinmayananda Mission at Powai and asked for protection and strength.

On my way back and in a reflective mood I wondered,

What is it about divorces, or is it simply human nature that we try and make the other person look bad? This is the man who I had shared my bed with, my dreams, and my innermost thoughts. He had seen me naked so many times, and I could have been the mother of his child if things had gone well between us. Didn't he know me inside out? He was talking this nonsense about me and sharing it with strangers. Since all of this was untrue, it hurt even more. On one hand they wanted me to be swathed, swamped and smothered in millions of layers of clothing touting their conservatism from the rooftops and on the other, they had wanted to set me out in the world to fend for myself. Then they aren't bothered about the men you might talk to.

After all, you are not their property/concern any more, so you can do what the hell you want to. It is a perverse definition of conservatism. Their theory seemed to be that as long as you are with me, you need to be completely covered away from the prying eyes of the public. But if I am not your self-anointed protector, I will strip you naked before I let you go. Where is the decency and humanity in this behaviour? It was unimaginable and hurtful like someone had yanked thirty teeth out of my mouth and forgotten to give me anaesthesia while doing so. Suddenly my thoughts were interrupted by Doshi promising to take me to a lawyer and some relative of his who was a counsellor in the family court.

But all I needed was some reassurance and love and there was no one to give that to me. I wanted my parents. How I missed my parents then and wished that they were alive. If you don't appreciate your parents try being an orphan for a few days and you'll know their value. When your gut is wrenched from inside you is how I felt when my divorce petition landed up and all the lies made me feel like a whore. I felt that my broken marriage was a personal failure and that I had to work hard on my life as it stood today and help myself. I have never felt more alone and lonely in my life.

That piece of paper I had in my hand represented my failure. I would be a public failure if my marriage failed. All my relatives would pronounce smugly, 'I told you so' coupled with the smirks, the sly sidelong glances reiterating that I am worthless. That piece of paper made me realize that I was alone again and was going uphill on an ever-winding road and chasing the mirage of togetherness. Till death do us apart seemed like a bad reality television show mocking my failure.

This paper in front confirmed it. It crushed my dreams of a secure planned future and hurled me into the choppy waters of an unplanned life where I would have to learn to swim again, and if I didn't learn, the chilly realization dawned on me that I'd just drown. I was angry and frustrated at the uncertainty of being thrown into the open without any safety net and my cocoon of a guaranteed life being ripped open and apart by the divorce petition. I'd have to restart again whether I liked it or not. Should I cry? No. I was persuading and promising myself to forget my pain and focus on a more positive path.

Then I snapped out of my reverie and reluctantly

looked at the date I had to appear in court. The first date was in Court Room No. 4, 4th Floor, Bandra. The day was the 4th of July, American Independence Day. Was it an omen that the courts would give me independence from all the T-H-A-P-A-K-S, the verbal, physical, mental and emotional abuse and enable me to become a superpower like America?

8

Kramer vs Kramer

B vs B sounded fantastic, like *Kramer vs. Kramer* that iconic movie. Am I a V/S, just a versus? So many years of screaming from the rooftops about my individuality and I am now a 'vs', with no other identity other than my husband being against me in a litigious court case he had initiated. I had come to the fourth floor and seen the name and number on a soft board and the divorce proceedings had reduced me to being a serial number and a vs—fantastic for my individuality.

The judge's courtroom was spacious—about 200 sq. ft. It had one entrance and a curtain at that entrance. On my right, sat a man who looked slimy and creepy. The judge's table looked huge and he was seated with his back towards the window but he had a pretty good view. There were two witness boxes—very *filmi*. The room was painted that indescribable colour that only government buildings have. It had a fan and since the windows were open it wasn't muggy and in fact was definitely clean and had no paan stains. Ooooh! The judge must be strict and a stickler to be able to get this done. The extreme left hand side had the sanctum sanctorum of the judge's chamber. The courtroom is important and imperative to the case as all the action has to take place here. It seemed pathetic to me as it had an air of finality and this is where it would all come apart.

As we entered the court the judge was already seated. He was in his uniform and looked impressive and formidable like his name and reputation, Judge Dhatrak. We entered and then stood reverentially. He asked me, 'Are you Mrs B?' I answered, 'Yes.' 'Where is your lawyer?' When I stood silently, he nodded in understanding. He said, 'Do you agree for a divorce?' I answered, 'No.' He asked the clerk to give us a date. We got one for four months later. I noticed my husband standing next to a lawyer who did not look so great. My husband looked through me at first and then when I walked up to him and his lawyer nodded imperceptibly, he greeted me. This seemed like a blood sport, like boxing where each punch at the other's psyche would get us a point.

Great! So now he needed a lawyer's permission to greet his wife. Did he seek his lawyer's or dad's or whoever's permission to bed me. I said, 'Do you want to go to the canteen?' His lawyer proceeded ahead and said that he'd call him. We went to the canteen on the first floor. It looked like an Udupi joint. He ordered a lassi and I asked for a cheese dosa and said, 'Why?' He said, 'Look, I can give it another chance but you know how it is.' I said in a begging tone, 'Let's go away to London and we can start life afresh. We both love each other and we can change a bit and forget the past. We can just be happy with whatever we can work and earn. Please, please let's give it another go.'

He said, 'I wish but you know the truth.' I said, 'Of course, I know.' His damn dad who would cut him off. He said, 'Do you have money?' I said, 'No, but you will give me a monthly maintenance when the court orders it and then an alimony.' He said, 'Not going to happen, da ...' and then checked himself in time, before he said dad. I said in anger, 'No, you are going to pay and there is a God up above and you wouldn't have dared to do this if my parents were alive and I know you will pay. I don't hate you or anything but you will be paying me.'

I thought even if I had been a whore and slept with someone so many times surely I would have made a fortune. Then I started begging him again to reconsider his decision or at least tell me what the real reason was. I met with a blank wall, which effectively translated to 'the family has decided'.

I finished my dosa and said, 'Bye, see you next time', like we were casually fixing up to meet for a romantic date, took an auto and went home. On the way back I thought about our wedding night. The bed was decorated with flowers and we had a curtain of marigold. It was beautiful. He approached me tentatively and I was wearing a sexy pink peignoir. He asked me whether I had protection. I told him, 'No' and I did feel coy. He kept one light on and we went to bed. His sexual abilities were like Maggi 2-minute noodles—2 minutes in and out, over and done with. Are men from rich families like that, that they don't feel the need to please their woman in bed, thinking that their money is enough for us to lavish all our love and sexiness on them? I wish if they had paid even a millionth of the attention to women as they did to their incomes, they would be such passionate lovers. But that day, the atmosphere was so romantic that I didn't mind. How would I have known that our love making would lead to war making in court and all that sex would yield zero money in court. Not that I was part of the whole romance and marriage for money. But surely you would expect something if your marriage went KAPUT.

I was a good wife. I kept a good home, looked after him, didn't create scenes, didn't spend too much of his money, made good food. Where Punjus live to eat not eat to live, I made pathetic chapattis, which looked variously like the map of India and Africa. But they can't deny paying me in court just because I made bad chapattis! For all that I had been to him, he didn't want to even give me enough money to support myself. I couldn't understand why. Because Simon says! I remembered the childhood nursery rhyme—Simon says, 'Stand,' and we all stood. Here I guess his daddy was Simon and was saying, 'Don't pay.'

I got home and Bobby was there and she gave me some tea and I just went to sleep. When I woke up in the evening I told Bobby what had happened and then went to my faithful Khar Gymkhana. I met a few friends there and told them, 'I have four months to get a lawyer. And nothing happened. We have to go for counselling next time, but I need the money. And I need money for a lawyer. If I don't have a lawyer, I can't get money from my hubby and if I don't have money, I can't get a lawyer—kind of circuitous, like the hen came first or the egg.' I got a few numbers from them and just begged off at 7 p.m. and headed home.

Next day I started the mega hunt for my lawyer. I was clear that I didn't want the divorce to be a protracted, bloody and messy battle hurting everyone in the bargain. I didn't want to hurl unnecessary ugly accusations which when they appear in paper in black and white in a petition written by lawyers cause irreparable damage to the psyche and people become cynical, angry and bitter by the time the divorce is over. I didn't want to be engaged in a WWE divorce battle with both of us jumping on each other with fake jungle cries, hitting and hurting each other mentally and proclaiming victory when in fact in a divorce there are no winners, except the lawyers who laugh all the way to the bank.

I started by calling two lawyers and the first one was the great Flavia Agnes who is a feminist and had fought her own case fantastically. She was busy and couldn't see me immediately so I rung up the other one. The next lawyer I spoke with agreed for an appointment and said that she would take the first fee when the first cheque from Paneer Boy arrived. And so with a steely resolve, an eye on my bank statement and pragmatism I went on to my next task

in hand, generating funds for the lawyer and for my life.
My attempts to do so were like a seventy-year-old firing
sexually into a twenty-year-old—vigorous but blank.

9

Adam, Eve, the Serpent . . .
Oops, the Lawyer

CASE NO# 12345 X vs Y is what I heard even though that was not what was called out.

Was I finally losing my mind or was I hallucinating and was cuckoo as my in-laws had so often said. Had they been right all along? No, unfortunately for them that wasn't the situation. The truth was more metaphorical than the actual reality. This is how a lawyer makes you feel when the case is going on—you are nothing but a case number. You may be a thick case number, a thin, a rich, a poor, a good, a bad, a problematic, or an easy one but you are only a case number. Your turbulent, traumatic married life gets filed as a case number to be flicked out each time there is preparation for your case.

While I was waiting for my name to be called out, I

took in the surroundings, my lawyer's office. It was just a normal office with comfortable waiting chairs, a reception area though there was no receptionist; I guess the interns did that job. There was a glass door at the entrance and another one which separated the lawyer's cabin from the reception. The flooring was wooden, which gave it a warm and welcoming look and God knows all us pariahs needed it especially, after being abandoned by our partners and subsequently a number of others.

The office was located close to the family court and it even had a small garden at its entrance which I again found very welcoming, and again, I thought, I needed the welcoming. I write this in the manner I remember though not in the order you usually observe things but my life wasn't exactly the most orderly. I had three or four glasses of water and thought, maybe nerves, which was natural in the situation and sat there drumming my fingers on my big handbag that had only little money. I wished it was the other way round.

Suddenly I heard a case number, or was it my name called out, and I was ushered into meet the lawyer. I entered the inner office and was greeted by a smiling lady and instantly I felt light and as if the gloom was shifting away. She greeted me with, 'How are you? Do you want some tea?' I nodded and marvelled at a lawyer who offered tea, and only later realized all this tea was in some parts definitely coming from my fee. The inner office again was done in wooden panelling and mirrors and glass with a plethora of thick law books which definitely impressed me and inspired faith. I thought, even if she has read half these books I am in safe hands. So there began my lawyer's journey into my life.

When the tea arrived, she asked me a bit about the case and to my utter horror, I started sobbing very loudly. I was just so relieved to be talking to someone who seemed to be a saviour after all the verbal beatings by relatives and others and the lies I had to feed everyone trying to pretend that all was well, that this simple enquiry just brought forth emotions like a black American Express card— UNLIMITED. I sobbed so much that she pushed the tissue box towards me and I used them quite generously. Then when I calmed down I thought, 'After all if the lawyer is going to charge me on an hourly basis I can't afford to be crying and paying for it because that would be cause for more crying—imagine an hourly rate for no advice but only the opportunity to cry.'

I then mentioned who I was married to and that the divorce petition had been filed and how the petition was a lie. She didn't ask me more but assured me, 'You have a good case, I have gone through some of your documents, we will win this case. Don't worry we will get you the best settlement.' I know this is probably the standard response for every one of their clients but at that time it was like rain in a desert—unexpected and welcoming and cooling. For once, since my petition was filed, I cracked a smile, a genuine one, not because of the money but because I didn't feel weak and helpless any more. I felt empowered. Surprisingly, a stranger made me feel that I wasn't alone any more and I had nothing to fear. It was like eating a scrumptious meal cooked lovingly by your mother after months of fasting, or getting the Liz Taylor–Richard Burton diamond after being dirt poor . . . you get the picture.

Then I took in the surroundings some more as she got some documents she had to sign, and realized that the atmosphere that was created, daintily, evoked faith and confidence in the clients. You definitely, didn't have to pretend to her, especially about wanting a settlement because it looked like she liked the good things in life and she wouldn't want you to go without them just because your spouse had decided to leave you high and dry.

Then came the difficult part. I asked her, or actually I told her, 'Currently I am not exactly flush with funds. Actually, I am broke. So I will have to pay you as soon as I can get a job,' and then started bawling again. I guess now that she knew that I was broke, the humiliation of telling her, a complete stranger that I had no funds overwhelmed me. It was really like the ultimate humiliation, like wearing high heels to impress a guy and then falling on him as soon as you enter the room where he is sitting because you lose your balance. I waited for her to tell me, 'Get out.' After all this was what quite a few people had done to me by then or maybe make me pay Rs 1000 for the rest of the tea. She smiled and said, 'Don't worry about that. We will settle the money when you get it.'

When I attempted to speak no words came out, but some fresh tears, though not the loud bawling of before. Guess I was all out of tears. At that time, I could have been her slave for life. I just thanked her graciously and requested her leave as I didn't want to impose more on her, as this was a free consultation and there is only so much you can or should take, without having much to offer back in return.

On the way back, I thought that I lucked out and maybe that the donations I made to causes I believed in, and some that I didn't even believe in, must have been paying me back with interest. For the first time in a long time I went back and slept like a baby and had no accompanying nightmares. I was set for now for the case.

But what really happened over a period of time was incomprehensible to me. When I started asking my lawyer about a few of the applications in our case that we should have won, she first became evasive and then condescending and told me that I wasn't a lawyer and she knew better. I wasn't a lawyer but I wasn't stupid. Then I started my own research, after all this was my case and I could look up judgements and orders. I was confident that based on the facts available with us, we should have won and started suspecting that my lawyer was throwing away my case. Since I had no concrete proof, but a strong gut feeling, I decided to continue with her as my lawyer. Then she started 'advising' me to settle the matter to which I was amenable to provided they apologized to me for the abysmal, shameful and cruel manner they had treated me. I didn't want their money. All I was asking for was an apology for all the pain they had caused me and for destroying my life and putting me through a grinder. I only wanted them to return the money which I had spent on the marriage. When she told me, quite sternly and irritatedly, that they were ready to do nothing of the sort, I stared at her in disbelief and her conduct became even more suspect in my eyes. Our productive, friendly meetings soon became silently vicious and completely non-productive. All the positivity and warmth was replaced by negativity and belligerence.

Finally, she suddenly started demanding huge amounts of money to represent me, despite knowing my precarious financial condition. When I paid some of it and asked for time to pay the rest, she just dropped my case. She wouldn't take my calls, wouldn't meet me when I went to her office and just became incommunicado. It was that simple, with no explanations given. It's as though she didn't want to represent me and was looking for some vague reason to not do so. Hiking up her fee provided her with the best way to get out of representing me. I wish she had been upfront and told me. Eventually, she just didn't turn up for a few of my court hearings and left me with no option but to speak my mind. I had to tell the judge, 'Sir I can't afford to pay my lawyer so she is not coming to court, can you tell her to.' He said, 'Madam, you would have to make a complaint about this, if you would like to pursue the matter about the lawyer's conduct.' I said, 'Your Honour, if I do that no one will ever represent me and am too emotionally weak at this moment.' He was kind enough or maybe had seen these situations often and so said, 'Take two months to find a lawyer.'

I went about lawyer hunting once again and this time I was a little more seasoned than when I had first started. After all, by now, I had already been in court for about five years. It wasn't that difficult, and as I understood, in long cases this does tend to happen as sometimes the lawyer asks to be excused and sometimes, the client just wants a change as she/he gets dissatisfied with the lawyer's expertise. Later, I discovered the reason for my first lawyer's shameful, unconscionable behaviour—she had sold out to my husband's side. There was never any concrete proof but the hallowed divorce walls were filled with murmurs of her latest sell-out or throwing a case. I just felt betrayed and it reiterated my previous notions of lawyers, that they are money-hungry and will even charge their own mother for making her will even if they are the beneficiary.

This notion would have continued till I met my new lawyer, Taubon Irani, who never spoke about money, never asked for a fee, was fair and even when she knew I had money and was too scared to part with it, insisted that I pay, only when I felt comfortable doing so. She represents you with her heart and for the joy of defending someone who is wronged. There are few like her but people like her definitely re-establish your faith in humanity and somewhere even redeem lawyers.

She was really a guiding light to me and provided a much needed balm to being left in the lurch by unscrupulous money-hungry lawyers. She was conscientious and practised law because she was passionate about it. I developed a close relationship with her, where I wasn't looking over my shoulder to check if my case had been compromised and was confident of her abilities and that she was batting in my corner and for my success in the case.

So I must admit, like any profession, lawyers also come as a mixed bag and maybe because their profession encourages it or maybe they have over a period of time learnt to ask for funds upfront and also because we perceive cases to be an unnecessary drain on our finances and hence we resent the lawyers much.

Even the long periods of time taken for a case add more to the anger at lawyers, as the end doesn't seem in sight and a case seems like a hydra-headed monster which seems to keep growing with each passing court date and we can't get to the bottom of it to put an end to it and we expect the lawyer to do it.

Whatever you do, please do ensure that you choose a lawyer who you can gel with and communicate with and who shares your core values as you may have difficulty in going with lawyers who want to put your spouse behind bars at the drop of a hat or drag your name through the papers and that may not exactly be your idea of fighting a case. I know it wasn't mine, so I never even entertained these ideas and in fact turned down a husband–wife lawyer couple who told me to do so.

I am presenting both sides of the coin to help you to decide what is best for you. Even when finding a lawyer it is best to go to the court and ask the clerks and peons there who are very helpful and always give the true picture without the smokescreen of diplomacy. In the family court, of course, the counsellors are also very forthright and frank. So word of mouth is the best way to check the credentials of a lawyer. Though the media also grants coverage to some lawyers, all of them may not be right for you; your lawyer has to suit your purpose and temperament.

My lawyer bailed me out of the difficult situation I was in and also helped me to cope emotionally and I must admit became, and is still, a good friend and I tell her she represents the rare category of lawyers and is like a character in a fairy tale—impossible to believe. She is an honest lawyer. Most of all, she wasn't a Shylock demanding money considering the stack of unpaid bills and huge zeroes that were there in my bank account.

10

Hard Cash or Hardly Cash

I was just staring, staring at the right hand side, the most important side to me now in my new state. The state where you wish, no one who you love, including yourself, lands up. The never-welcoming situation which you wish will go away sooner than you can say Jack Robinson. The precarious condition which you have no control over and is more often than not forced upon you. The state of impoverished finances. Broke, poor, not so rich, depleted finances or whatever delicate euphemism you want to use. The right side that I am staring at, wishing it would be all zeroes, are the prices on the menu.

Your social life doesn't become a zing just because you are going through the D word but you have to be careful who you go out with otherwise the tongues will wag and another wagging will be your lawyer, wagging a finger of disapproval and another one the judge, wagging his head in the negative when listening to your defence or even granting you an interim maintenance. I did go out with college friends who had known me for ages, both men and women. The guys a little more, as guys also are more apt to listen and I was closer to them, and also, well let's face it, in the current circumstances, to pay. Did I take advantage of the guys coercing them even subtly to pay? I must admit I am guilty but at least I did it to guys who I knew could afford to pay. Besides, most of them were my friends and would have paid anyway.

I remember when I first moved (a euphemism for getting kicked out) out of my husband's house, my help, Bobby, helped me so much financially. She was a star and even offered not to take any salary. I did for a couple of months avail of that offer but once I got the money I paid her. It's funny how the most unlikely people help you out. She really did look after me and I am eternally grateful to her. So at least humanity is not dictated by finances.

The first money that I earned didn't come from a job but from Zaveri bazaar. I went there and flogged my mangal sutra, a piece of jewellery that is the mark of a married woman and some other jewellery that had been given to me by my husband. What was the point of the mangal sutra if the spirit behind it didn't exist? Wearing any visible marks of his presence were pointless, at this stage. It was definitely a practical thing to do; after all, can you really eat gold to satisfy your hunger?

After this I was alright financially for some time and

much later, got a job. But still it was goodbye to Parisian perfumes and hello to attar. No more La Senza and Victoria's Secret but a big embrace to Maiden Form lingerie. Fancy footwear was of course out of the question and for once in my life I was happy that Bata shoes and sandals not only made your feet look like blocks of wood but also last as long as a tree.

Bye bye Taj and Maratha Sheraton and a sweet hi to Taja and Sharaton, the fake variety. MH02K 2339, my old car that I could have kept in a museum, was just lying unused but all the other MHO2 S were being heavily utilized. Yes, I had become an expert at taking autos. The petrol cost wasn't high for the car but the less I ran it the lesser I had to spend on the maintenance. I was happy that I had a glowing skin so had almost no expense on cosmetics.

My clothes were really stylish, if you ignored the fact that they were fashionable . . . a few seasons ago. Every day was a tough battle and my best friend was the calculator. I'm sure I must be having recessive Gujarati genes and they became my dominant genes in these tough financial times to still survive and thrive. Or maybe I am a thoroughbred Gujarati and my mum hid the fact from me!

My house showed the ravages of time and absence of money for its upkeep. I think all my creativity was put to test just to make it presentable. First, it badly needed painting. I had no money for that, remember I had to fill my tummy first. I just used about eight cans of spray paint and made the sun and mountains and a river on the main wall of the living room. I painted my room pink, wherever the plaster was peeling off and also made a few hearts for lightening up the room.

Finally in the next room I made all sorts of food objects like grapes and oranges on the wall and just spray painted again where the paint was peeling. The mosaic tiles which were filthy I just covered with cheap durries (cotton rugs). So at least the room looked bright and cheery. Finally, the old windows were covered with curtains using my wedding sarees; they were heavy and had all sorts of gold embroidery on them so the room really looked rich. There is much you can do if you put your mind to it. Although this did not change my reality but it sure as hell made it look prettier and snazzy.

Namrita, who came to the house as a substitute help brought me back crashing to earth by remarking, 'Didi, these tiles are really old and dirty. Why don't you change them?' I went ballistic on her and said, 'If you are so concerned about my well-being, why don't you sacrifice your salary and I'll use that money.' But it was the truth—I really did need cash. I felt pathetic about snapping, and apologized to her. Why blame her? She was after all stating the truth about the impoverished state of my finances. I did think of various ways of supplementing my income and ended up taking English tuitions for some children.

While mentioning my impoverished state to a friend's friend who was in advertising, he recommended that I should take his overseas clients out for sightseeing and the agency would pay me. It sounded suspiciously like being an escort and I didn't know whether there was sex

involved but I felt and knew that this was not the way
to do things. There had to be respectable ways of making
money. Otherwise it would be easy to sell your dignity to
make quick money. Sometimes the enthusiasm of friends
is so misplaced.

I wish, in desperate times, that I had been smart and
taken the money from my husband's coffers when I had
the opportunity. I wish I had collected the sarees and other
parts of my trousseau from their house. When I was asked
to leave my in-laws' house I had billions with me because
at least I was alive and had my dreams which were priceless.
The grand total in money that was in my bank account
wouldn't even be enough to cover a dinner date for two
at a restaurant near the family court. Let the drums roll as
I tell you the exact amount in my account—the princely
sum of SEVEN HUNDRED AND FIFTY RUPEES!

11

My First Date

Dinner, dancing, romance, kissing, hugs. That's what usually happens on a date, right? But this was a date with a difference. So there I was, in my twenties, with no job, no parents, no postgraduate professional qualifications, not enough money but lots of friends. In short, I was in 100 degrees of deep shit, would've been in 200 degrees of deeper shit if I had no friends. For now, all I could do is concentrate on my latest date. The night before, I would have liked to drink myself senseless, slip into a stupor and never ever wake up again.

Dark thoughts were a constant litany in my mind. Oh delightful death . . . why do you elude me so . . . carry me into your ample bosom and fly me to the heavens where I'll sob in my parents' arms . . . set me free from this skulduggery . . . let this be an unreal nightmare which vanishes when I wake up.

But I remembered I had told myself to be positive and let's face it, I'd have lost out on what till now had been a great life and was also sure the opposite party would be only too happy to see me go to hell. We were the opposite sides now. This is the harsh reality of divorce. One day you are sharing a bed, naked in each other's arms and the next day you are on opposite sides.

I took one third of .25 mg of a sleeping tablet and drifted off into slumberland. Was it a good sleep, surprisingly it was. Woke up refreshed and was ready to take on the world. I wore white clothes, an old tattered salwar kameez, white the colour of widows and I was one. After all, when the man who is supposed to protect you not only abandons you but also attacks, you are a widow. For all practical purposes, your husband is dead. I did feel a bit manic putting on a fake smile to combat the apprehension within. So the white bordering on yellow clothes (which were to become my uniform in court) was what reflected my inner turmoil. Shattered and tattered inside and out. This was a disaster as I was never shabbily dressed but was sensible enough to know that I had to look depressed. I didn't have to try hard—every bone in my body reflected my mental state.

That morning, I said my prayers, faithful Bobby praying along with me and then plying me with food. At 9.45 a.m. I was on my way to the family court. I went to the court in an auto, not my car, because it would look improper that at some stage I would be asking for money from my spouse and then land up in the car to ask for it. Besides, I never had enough money to maintain the car, so auto it was. I didn't notice the time it took to get there but was there on time. I asked around for the family court in Bandra East and then finally landed at my destination.

I took one look at the building and it was disgusting, like the ideologies of my in-laws which they had instilled in their son. I didn't hate them—I just didn't understand them and I still don't. I have no reason to hate them and besides, grudges and hate are just unnecessary emotions and a waste of your good positive vibes. I entered with the trepidation akin to a virgin going away for a dirty weekend for the first time—inexperienced, smiling self-consciously at everyone, casting sidelong glances to see if anyone was looking at you. A certain amount of guilt at being in a court filled my heart, as though just by being here I was a criminal. I climbed the stairs and reached the landing outside the lift. The building had peeling paint of an indescribable colour and definitely had paan stains at the corners. So in short, it was a typical government office.

I stood in the queue outside the lift and the queue already had 10–15 people. There were three lifts, two for litigants and one for lawyers. My turn came after two turns as only five could go in a shot. I got in and was engulfed and enveloped by sandalwood incense and smoke. I understood another Indian syndrome—praying to gods, even in a lift. Wearing our spirituality on our sleeves is reflected in loudspeakers at every neighbourhood religious gathering, with the women singing their guts out tunelessly so that even a deaf man's ears would bleed, or maybe they think God is deaf.

The peon or the liftman, a sure sign of hidden unemployment in the country, had the sandalwood and *sindoor*, vermillion, smeared on his forehead. He was wearing a Gandhi cap and the whitish government uniform and had a buck-toothed smile reserved for ladieshhhh (this was his pronunciation for us ladies) and was skinny as hell and had a wheatish complexion. His cheerful demeanour made me smile and he announced loudly that the lift does not stop at the first floor.

I got off at the fourth floor and was again assaulted by the overwhelming stench of the loos—an Indian or Indian subcontinent phenomenon. The humour of it struck me; all our relationships were going down the toilet, leaving a bad stench behind. I had finally found something to cheer me up. I entered the seating area outside the courtroom and saw benches, like in schools, arranged from one end of the room to the other end, for seating the litigants. These were arranged in three rows and most of them were occupied. Everyone looked sad. The fan wasn't cool enough and it was muggy in Mumbai. I noticed paan stains in the corners. The people again caught my eye and I wondered were they really sad or had I projected my sadness on them. Freud would've been happy with my astute observations. They were accompanied by friends, family, lawyers and I was alone but I knew I was in it to win it, or at least that's what I kept on telling myself to provide strength to myself. On one side, adjoining each other were the counsellors' rooms which proudly proclaimed their names.

I looked again at the judge's room and wondered what

had brought me here. Why was I standing in this room which had paan stains and was stuffy and I wanted to run, perhaps both showed the state of our relationship—we needed to get out of it because we were constricted in it and we spat it out, the red stains were definitely our blood. I didn't understand the reason and according to me the relationship, however bad it seemed, definitely did not merit a legal KAPUT. Divorce for me was an ugly word that no one in a marriage or outside of it, wanted to hear. Even if you read about serial marriers and divorcers, they like getting married and not divorced. One of my friends who married four times will happily tell you this. Despite all my pretensions, which I realized only then, of being forward thinking and the entire razzmatazz that goes with it, I just didn't want to end up having notched a divorce to my credit in my twenties and that too after barely making the one year plus mark.

So why did the relationship sour? I think one can never fully know why and the multitude of reasons all add up one fine day to complete the jigsaw called broken relationships. The reasons can be as much as verbal abuse to physical abuse, to something like a changing job, an affair or even a downturn in business, realizing that you want different things in life. In my case, I don't know the exact reason besides wanting different things, physical abuse and a general feeling of me being stifled and treated like a stray dog. But did it warrant a divorce? In my opinion—no! A big resounding, 'No!' Paneer Boy and I could've sorted it out, I felt—or at least at that time.

Maybe if we had started our life independently as an upwardly mobile couple without the hawk-like observation of Prem Cheapda or the constant unnecessary guidance of everyone or the interference from all the so-called well-wishers . . . well, no point crying over spilt milk. The reality was that I was in court with my husband having filed for divorce from me because he (and his entire coterie) wanted this marriage to end.

Suddenly I was back to the present and my thoughts were interrupted by the querulous jarring voice of the peon who had asked one lady to get off the seat which belonged to a cop. I stood and looked at these people who had lost out on love and maybe some would or had found love again. I saw aunties with their heaving bosoms cursing God who had accompanied their young girls and then realized why all the seats were taken. Because in India, marriage is an occasion where everyone is a stakeholder. There is a *band, baaja, baraat* in marriage; similarly in the court as your parents, assorted relatives and family friends accompany you to the court so it's a *dhoom dhadaka* divorce.

I really had no one at every step of my divorce. It made me feel even worse and I experienced an acute loneliness. But then we come and go alone in this world. Even then I had a burning desire to take over and undo the wrong and just plough ahead and carve a new path ahead scattered with nuggets of bravery and passion.

I wondered then what I had that they really wanted from me. They definitely wanted the divorce and for that they should pay me. I decided I would use the money and move overseas. I thought of asking for twenty-five lakhs as that is what an immigration to Australia would cost. I would study in Australia and definitely get a job. This would be behind me and well I don't want to think about what will happen in my personal life, frankly speaking I don't care. Just an escapism from the actual facts and as I tried to put maximum space between me and the unpleasant incident, an actual, physical gap thinking that this will help me to heal. Literally like leaving my old life behind and running away into another one. It would help.

The dull white interiors added to the funeral-like state of my mind—they looked like creepy crawlies that wanted your life but they wouldn't get mine. Some of the people looked so devastated that I wanted to console them. I wondered what I looked like—sad, happy, relieved, intelligent, sexy, pretty, ugly when my inner voice was rudely interrupted by the same jarring voice saying, 'Paneer Boy B vs Vandana B, Paneer Boy B vs Vandana B.'

12

Intercourse Maintenance

When does a bitter pill taste like heaven? When does a cabbage diet taste like a McDonalds combo? Are these things possible, or are they like unicorns, just pure figments of our imagination? Yes, these experiences are more than possible. I lived through them.

I was in court, chatting with the peon, waiting for my turn. This felt like my first date because I was going to court filled with sky-high expectations, like a child who expects the world from her parents. I already had attended a couple of court dates, and the judge had sent Paneer Boy and me to the court marriage counsellor who had also put an F in the report card of our marriage. The case had gone on to the next logical level but this was the day for the hearing of the intercourse, oops interim maintenance. I was also going with my legal bodyguard, my lawyer.

Paneer Boy was looking very glum and he was, as usual, avoiding me. I did not understand this behaviour at all. They were the ones that filed for divorce. Wasn't it my right to contest it or did they want me to just be a doormat even here? Shouldn't I even speak up against what I felt was unjustified behaviour against me? I didn't want to divorce him and he was angry about that and that would reflect in his scowling, at times depressed, expression which made him look like the Grim Reaper. In a way, he was really death itself, at least for this relationship.

Our turn was called out and we entered the courtroom. The judge announced that we need to be putting forth our case for interim maintenance. As always, his lawyer began by asking for more time to prepare their case. The judge sternly refused, stating that they had already taken up too much time. I wanted to get up and hug the judge instantly.

His lawyer opened the argument and said, 'Your Honour, we want to bring to your notice the sufficient wealth that the respondent has. She doesn't deserve any interim maintenance. She has a house of her own and is well educated. She has enough skills to earn her own money. She is qualified and has worked before—she should have no difficulty getting a job. She has ancestral land in Himachal Pradesh worth crores and she also has sold some other property in Haryana. She also has a lot of jewellery given by my client and by her mother.'

Listening to him, I thought that if I was indeed so fantastic and accomplished as he was painting me out to be, I should be awarded 'wife of the year' instead of being rewarded with a divorce. I marvelled at the ludicrousness of their claims of selling property in various parts of the country because if I had actually sold them then I wouldn't have to stand there with a begging bowl. The truth was really much bleaker and my financial position was pathetic, to say the least. The property in Himachal Pradesh was a piece of land which my father had invested in on faith and which turned out to be barren land—far from the lucrative apple orchard that he believed he was buying.

The judge replied, 'That is *streedhan* [brideprice] and cannot be taken into account for wealth, especially the jewellery given by her mother. Surely you are aware of the law?'

By this point, I was loving the judge and kissed him mentally!

The lawyer continued his arguments saying, 'She also has not been a good wife and has . . .' but the judge interrupted him angrily and said, 'Are you not aware of the law? This is a hearing for interim maintenance and not for deciding the case on its merits. Stick to the points under discussion!'

The lawyer began again and said, 'Sorry, Your Honour. We have also asked for credit card statements and also the bank statements from her and also the phone, electricity and mobile phone bills to determine her financial position.'

The judge by now was bellowing and said, 'Which court do you practise in? You cannot ask for these documents now—it is too late. You are supposed to procure and produce them in court on the day the matter is being presented. If you do not have them, I will have to proceed further. Before you ask me for more time, I will not be giving you another date. You have delayed the matter enough.'

The judge could clearly see through their deceitful delaying tactics, as transparent as a Bollywood heroine's white see-through saree in a rain sequence, and that their case had more holes than a piece of cheese. In short, their case had no merits, it was weak and they were only using the court as an excuse for avoiding any legal justice.

Paneer Boy's lawyer tried to persuade and request the judge to change his mind but the judge wouldn't be moved and said, 'Please proceed further. I have a number of other matters at hand today.' The lawyer, having no option, summing up his extremely weak argument said, 'Keeping all these facts in mind I would request you not to grant her any maintenance.'

However, I had already tuned out by then and kept thinking a court date was finally looking good for me. Maybe today God was smiling at me. I came back to reality to hear my lawyer address the judge, 'Your Honour, my client had requested for phone bills and others which we have got. I would like to draw your attention to the fact that my client has never denied that she has her own house but she also needs money to live which the house cannot provide her. She is educated but at the insistence of the petitioner, she has given up her career a few years ago and now has to upgrade her skills before she can get another job. However, she is too traumatized at the moment to even think of employment. Her land in Himachal is a joint property and is difficult to sell. Currently, my client, an orphan, has no means of supporting herself.'

But listening to my lawyer I really did feel bad for myself. Whatever she had said was the truth and if you took away my bravery from the equation, you really would pity me. Looking back, I don't know how I kept going in those days and was willing to take risks bordering on the foolish. I would've gone to any lengths to survive with self-respect.

The judge started dictating the judgement order immediately, which was quite unusual, and said, 'I am ordering you to pay her an interim maintenance of Rs 12000 a month starting from the month of September. Failure to do so will lead to the dismissal of your petition.' Paneer Boy's lawyer interrupted saying, 'My client has lent money to his father and also has pending dues of about Rs 47,000 on his credit card.'

The judge, who was quite irritated by the overbearing attitude of Paneer Boy's lawyer and by the lack of courtroom decorum, responded with a legal admonishment, 'Do not interrupt me when I am dictating a judgement. I will hold you in contempt of court for it! Your client lending his father money is an internal matter and has no bearing. If he has Rs 47,000 to spend on a credit card then perhaps I should order a higher maintenance.'

I saw Paneer Boy staring open-mouthed at the judge as though he had actually seen an alien! He simply could not believe that he would have to pay me monthly maintenance—I who was, in his opinion, the biggest loser,

slut, nobody, a human dreg worse than the dirt beneath his
feet, a NOTHING . . . you get the drift, in the world would
have to be paid by HIM—the omnipotent, all powerful
master. I visualized him clutching his heart when the order
was being dictated. I ran my eyes over his face and feared
that maybe he was having a heart attack. I'm sure this
was actually the entire family's typical reaction whenever
they had to pay money to anyone, and it would especially
hurt to pay me—the woman unworthy of their beloved
son. I smiled inwardly. They had surely paid the lawyer an
arm and a leg but for the soon-to-be-ex-member of their
family, they were ready to give her nothing.

I am sure their reaction to the order for interim
maintenance was exacerbated by the fact that they would
have to give me this money that I didn't have to account
for right down to the last paisa. No taunts would be made
when the money was handed over and there would finally
be no Lord and Master scenario. He was, needless to say,
cast in that role of the Lord and Master of the marital
Universe and I was the lowly slave, who was doled out
money for running the house and relegated to doing all
the inconsequential things.

I felt like running up to the judge's chair, embracing
him and saying, 'Oh Judge saab, where have you been all
my life? You are my knight in shining armour and have
freed me.'

I cannot describe how happy I was hearing this judgement.
It wasn't just about the money but was about validating that
I wasn't wrong and they didn't do right by me. It was a

vindication, the first of many that you have to stand up to the wrong even if you are weak because ultimately there is justice. It also injected a healthy dose of positivity in my life that finally something was going my way.

Paneer boy looked like curdled milk. His scowl was now focused on his lawyer and for once, I wasn't the object of his contempt. I thought that they would now change their lawyer because it certainly looked like this one wasn't particularly useful. The funny part was that the judge ordered maintenance to start from September but the court clerk typed August onto the order. And so, I would be paid for an extra month. The judge also ordered a payment of Rs 10,000 to my lawyer from which she would get her first instalment of fees. I wondered then if this day could get any better. The events of this day had only strengthened my belief in the fact that truth always triumphs and you get your reward if you stick to the truth.

But do you think, after the court order, they paid maintenance without making a fuss?

No, of course, they wouldn't pay. After all, Prem Cheapda didn't need to play by the rules. He believed he owned the world and he would decide when or what to do. But he was so, so wrong. At the next date in court, we filed a claim for the money due to me. The judge told them to deposit the money with my lawyer before the end of the day or their petition would be dismissed. They tried to make some excuses about how little time was granted to pay or the payment amount being too high but the judge was having none of it and said, 'You were given adequate time.

You live in Pali Hill and I am sure you have at least this much money to pay your wife. You are only using delay tactics. You must pay in time or face the consequences. She can even move the court for an arrest warrant.' Hearing this, PB's face went as white as a ghost and he sprang into action like a bullet through a gun.

I'm sure Paneer Boy must've rushed to Daddy because, by the evening, he had paid the amount to my lawyer. I am sure that was the day he must've felt like slicing me into little bits and feeding me to the dogs. He loved his money and didn't like paying anyone. To pay a wife who wasn't serving and servicing him, but was in court, was like giving away money unnecessarily. He was really upset.

This was only the first instance. Over time, Paneer Boy and his family delayed paying me maintenance a number of times. The process of asking for it in court was replayed each time, and each time I could feel his hatred and anger towards me get magnified by the fact that he had to pay and maintain his still-legally wedded wife.

This Rs 12, 000 that I got from Paneer Boy made me feel richer than Bill Gates and Steve Jobs rolled into one, not because it was a bank breaking amount, but because I got a colossal slice of hope. I was sure with this money even if I went on a *karela* (bitter gourd) juice diet, it would taste fantastic. And I was sure that my friends, being generous as they are, would even share this bitter concoction with me, as they had walked beside me, holding me every step of the way, showering unconditional love as only a parent can, in this traumatic journey so far.

13

My Friends, My Angels

Leaning on each other, and providing a shoulder to cry on—my friends were always there for me. They were angelic, helpful, honest without being cruel, available at all times and most of all, non-judgemental. I hate judging people or being judged as a norm, but I hated it even more during those years. When you are going through a divorce, even before you know it, without figuring out all the facts, people will judge you. The man who leaves is a bastard, a Casanova and the woman asking for her rights is a greedy bitch, a slut.

Why can't it be that people have started disagreeing with each other and that years of living together have forced them to realize that they are not meant to be together? Why can't it just be as simple as that? When my friends embraced me whole-heartedly during this struggle and

107

offered no opinions or judgements, I cried with joy. They just welcomed me back into their midst, never asked any awkward questions and offered nothing but unconditional acceptance.

I was able to call them no matter what time of day or night and talk about my fears. I was terrified that I would be left penniless by my in-laws and would not even be able to pay my lawyer. I feared losing everything, including my reputation, which the divorce petition had already ensured was in shreds. I was plagued by insecurities. I talked incessantly about the stigma of divorce and rued the fact that even though I was young, no one would ever want to be with me any more and constantly feared that my in-laws were spying on me.

My fears were not unfounded when I actually saw and heard one of the managers from the Khar Gymkhana Club making a call to my in-laws. I suspected he was reporting to my father-in-law about my comings and goings and my companions. I was fed up with them and their deviousness and so we planned to trap their spy. My friends and I would pretend that I had an active social life and would insinuate that I was seeing a lot of men. We would then see him going to make the call. To ensure that we were right, we also let it slip that I was going out of town. Sure enough, for a few days, I saw shadowy figures near my house, watching my movements, and I knew I was right.

But I had no way to get these people to stop. A dear friend came up with a novel solution. She confronted the manager at the Khar Gymkhana and said, 'Sudhakar, you have known me since I was a kid.' He nodded amiably and looked at her indulgently as one looks at a daughter. She said, 'You also know that I know how to deal with people who are nasty to me or my friends.'

Sudhakar, who had no idea where this conversation was going, continued to listen. She continued, 'You have been spying on Vandana and I know that for a fact so don't deny it. I want to tell you that if you continue this, I will have to be very mean and vile to you.' At this point, he looked scared. She then told him that he would have to do what she was telling him. We planned for Sudhakar to carry information back to my in-laws saying I would not be appearing in court for some time. We also had him tell them that I was planning to back out of the case.

As a result of this, a rookie lawyer from their lawyer's office came to court without full information on the case. The judge ordered him to pay the interim maintenance and he was completely lost! The judge told him that if the client didn't pay, he would be in contempt of court. I think the poor guy was so petrified he was willing to pay out of his own pocket. For a lawyer to want to do that, you can imagine the fear! But my in-laws paid the money all the same.

We started sending completely incorrect information until one day, finally, we had Sudhakar tell my in-laws that I was becoming deeply religious and was likely to renounce the world. I thought that it would be very obvious that this information was worth its weight in crap but they were so paranoid that they believed everything. It was hilarious especially when I ended up at the court wearing a tulsi mala and they looked at me, hawk-like, hoping that I'd withdraw from the case as I was turning into a sanyasin—but no such luck for them. I just dug my heels in and stayed.

It was clear to me that all of this was going well because of my friends. They protected me like a mother would protect her young. They even offered me money but I usually refused. But they took care of me in so many other ways like paying for meals, buying me gifts, usually unasked. Their generosity really warmed me.

Despite being an orphan, I had these people as my family and what a family it was! I loved and cherished them as they did me. Of course, they all had their faults as did I but these were the best friends I could ever have asked for.

My friends gathered around me and helped me get a new job, a new life and insisted that I dress my age. They told me I wasn't a widow, just a young person going through divorce. They prevented me from slipping into depression and even if I did, they propped me up. The best part is that they were there, and not just pretending to be there—physically and emotionally available to me. I had my case and my friends helping me through it and while I wasn't obsessed about it any more, I did fear that I would lose. But thanks to the emotional support of friends I was able to carry on with my life as best as possible. I had gone from existing and surviving to LIVING.

The same friends were mentioned in the petition as lovers. If all of them were my lovers, what was I doing being married to someone else? I would have been busy for years with my lovers alone! In fact, it became a joke with my friends; saying that if they didn't concede to my demands, I would make them famous by including them in my petition. Since a number of my friends were men, I was asked constantly how I handled these friendships and if a guy and a woman could really be friends? Or is it always friends with benefits or fuck buddies?

In this day and age, these were redundant questions. I personally think that it would have been different when we lived in a more restricted society but at least in the bigger cities in most situations, men and women can be just friends. Sure you can be attracted to a friend who is of the opposite sex but you don't always act on it, After all, we don't always act on our primal instincts. You know, sometimes I've found it's easier to deal with someone of the opposite sex because there are fewer complications, no rivalry, mutual appreciation and a different perspective—a perfect potpourri for friendship.

One particular incident always stands out in my memory. I was up late one night, chatting with my friend, Sid. We continued talking for about two hours and it was 5 a.m. when we finished talking! Knowing it was a Saturday the next day and that I would sleep, I yawned loudly and said I'd sleep for at least ten hours. He wished me a good night and asked if I'd need him for the next four hours. Teasingly I asked him if he was fed up of me already when he said that he was going to Kolkata to visit his parents for the weekend and would be in the plane if I needed him during that time.

I felt so guilty about depriving him of sleep and having robbed him of precious time with his parents because he would now be exhausted when he got to Kolkata and he'd have to sleep. I apologized quietly and he laughed and told me not to be silly! I felt more than a bit ecstatic and proud for having such great friends; no one could take them away from me.

This incident with Sid led me to think that there must be so many people in the same predicament as me, and perhaps a number of them didn't have a great support system of friends and non-judgemental people to take them through. How must they be managing—lonely or worse still, getting bad advice with no one there for them. They must be miserable and possibly also on the wrong track. I kept wondering how they would be getting their information and about who would be guiding them. Worst of all, they must be so fed up of being advised and judged.

I started empathizing with them and knew I had to do something for them. If it were not for my friends, I would never have got to the next big thing in my life which not only helped hundreds of people, but was also the first step to healing me and perhaps changing my life. My friends were my angels and they helped me to create a 360 Degrees angel which helped to heal and give strength to people going through divorce.

14

Suicide Prevention and More

'Vandana, I have had enough and I am going to kill myself,' said the alarmingly cold voice at the other end of the phone. It was my friend from the divorce group. In a calm voice, I said, 'Hang in there, your order is coming through and you can't let them win.' She just sobbed and then her voice choked in an attempt to say something, but she couldn't say anything and just sobbed some more. So I finally said, 'At least listen to what I have to say and then go ahead and do what you want.'

So I set off to Andheri to meet her and offer whatever little comfort I could. She, you see, was a member of 360 Degrees Back to Life, the support group that I had started—the first and only support group in India for people going through divorce. The main aim of the group is to provide non-judgemental support to those going through divorce and also provide guidance about the entire procedure of divorce. So with this aim, which evolved over time, the support group took off.

During my conversation with Sid, I realized that people who weren't as extroverted as me and who had very few people to count on or even talk to would be incredibly lonely. Besides they may not even have a good friend who would listen with endless patience, offer a shoulder to cry on and support them unconditionally without expecting anything in return.

Soon after, I said to myself, 'Let's see if we all divorcees or those in the middle of a divorce can get together and chat. Isn't it possible for us to meet and say silly, stupid, funny things about our soon-to-be former in-laws, and exchange gossip about lawyers and alimony? The group could be a forum to share our funny, stupid thoughts, secret desires and the frustrations of our experiences. These would help us retreat into a non-morbid reality and have harmless fun in our life. This is very important while being weighed down by the drudgery of divorce. Most of these meetings offered an escape into a fantasy world where we were happy and prancing about without a care in the world.

And so, the group 360 Degrees Back to Life was officially born around 2001. It was so named because all of us members started from a point 0 and went through the entire learning experience of divorce to complete an entire cycle and reach 360 degrees from where we start our life afresh. We then restart our new life from new point of reference, richer with our life experiences we proceed to carve out a new successful path for ourselves—a whole new bright shiny life where we are superstars.

The group started without any core committee, a hierarchy or even membership fees. 360 Degrees Back to Life was just like a normal group of friends meeting up and catching up on life. The group didn't have an office, and besides, who wanted to meet in the office? We met for coffees and dinners and just friendly outings where we all paid our own bills.

When we met, we each spoke about our case and no one offered any unsolicited advice but just listened. It is a relief to unburden yourself not only to someone who offers no advice but is also non-judgemental and can empathize because they are in the same predicament. Interestingly, the one thing all of us agreed on was that we would not meet in places that could be construed as shady and that we would not meet for the purposes of a hook-up. Anyway, at that stage of our lives, if anyone had even suggested being in another relationship, we would have all vomited at the unpalatability of this advice.

Along with group meetings, I also had individual meetings for those who wanted them. A typical one-on-one meeting involved discussing the stage of a person's case, the logistics of organizing money for further proceedings, dealing with the lawyer, career advice and options. We also discussed issues like dealing with the general bitchiness of relatives, in-laws and their weird behaviour, the pressure on your parents, sometimes the pressure by the parents, the suffering of the couple's children, and frustration with the legal system. Amazingly, most of these discussions have not only provided solace but also solutions.

Initially I used to conduct these meetings as an one-on-one, but as the group grew, these counselling sessions happened over email, in large groups, and in interactive sessions organized by a few Embassies and other organizations. Sometimes all I did was put one member in touch with the other to provide solace to each other. We became links in a chain—each supporting and increasing the strength of the other.

The group also compiled lists of good lawyers which was very useful to members. We also helped each other find jobs or through the legalese involved in divorce. The members of the group were also counsellors of sorts and we would listen empathetically to each other. The best part is that 360 Degrees Back to Life was and is still free. The group does take donations but these are always voluntary and the funds are used for the members of the group.

So we met, talked and vented and got some legal solutions and helped heal each other. Mostly though, it was the talking that was therapeutic. Some of us even went to court with another person if they were scared to face their court date. That's not bad for an organization that has no money and no fixed membership. At that stage, we didn't even realize that we were counselling and acting as pillars of support for each other. We were just venting and sharing our experiences since we were all going through the same thing.

Personally, I'm sure we dropped 360 kg of emotional baggage after each meeting as we unburdened all our woes—

everything connected with our lives at the moment was dominated by divorce. Our faces shone with happiness each time we met. I didn't make any specific plans for the future of the support group because I didn't know that it would be so successful. In fact, the success of the group took me by complete surprise. It was only when it continued to flourish that I started making notes about what exactly we were doing—what were our feelings, what were our needs and what exactly did we want as people/litigants going through divorce. Most of these notes have even come handy when I started penning this divorcologue. 360 Degrees provided me the starting point for this book.

The success of **360 Degrees Back to Life** proves the innate need of people to talk and have someone to listen to, providing non-judgemental support. The group has counselled so many people and saved marriages because in the support group, we look at divorce as the last option. We do not promote divorce, but if you are going to get divorced you must get into the proceedings somewhat prepared. Divorce is not for the fainthearted and somewhere I know from the voices I hear that we have made a difference to a number of lives. The voices are straight from the heart and have struck a chord with me through emails, meetings and even handwritten notes, which I am sharing with you in the appendix of the book. When you read them, you may be able to understand the passion behind my work.

I keep getting asked why I don't get organizational donations or support for the group. Earlier, it was simple—I didn't need it. But now when I do, I just don't get it. The reason, stated clearly by a friend in one of the foreign embassies in Mumbai, is that no one wants to be associated with the cause of divorce. I've said this even before, which of course keeps me moving ahead for this cause. Why do I do it? Perhaps because I feel no one should suffer as much as I did and even if they do, they must be helped in their attempt to make some sort of a life for themselves. Perhaps I am foolish and idealistic and feel I have to keep working at something that no one wants to work for. I have been told innumerable times that I am stupid for working so hard for this cause and if I had pursued something else, I would have been rich and famous. But passions are something that happen and you can't help what you are passionate about. Couple it with an indefatigable will and that's a killer combination.

The reason for the success of the group was that it is India's first and only group for people going through divorce. It provides non-judgemental support to those going through divorce and its membership is free. Most of all—it provides empathy and I am not someone preaching and downloading from a higher plane but from the same predicament as I myself am going through a divorce. I use the term divorce and no foolish euphemisms like separation and taking time off because I along with the group work towards eliminating the stigma surrounding and clouding divorce.

The only regrettable part of the group is that we hardly have any permanent members, because when people's divorces are over, they move on and sometimes, do not even keep in touch. It's like we are able to provide guidance and support but we aren't able to provide a solution to the stigma of divorce. Once they are done with their case, they don't want to be associated with the group. But I look at it like a mother who wants to heal her kids and let them fly without any other expectations. After all, 360 Degrees Back to Life is perhaps the rare non-judgemental support system they will know in this tough socio-legal battle. And despite very few permanent members, for many people, 360 Degrees Back to Life became a chosen family instead of the one they were born into.

15

Statutory Warning: Relatives Are Injurious to Health

I firmly believe that the number of relatives you have is directly related to your success—the more the success, the more the relatives. Like they say, you can choose your friends not your relatives. My thoughts are based on my experiences. In fact, after speaking to so many friends and acquaintances, I realize I am not alone in feeling this way.

When the divorce petition came, my relatives started coercing me to grant the divorce. They just didn't want to hear my side of the story. The worst was that you expect your well-wishers to side with you, but far from that, my relatives didn't even want to hear my side of the story. In fact, they decided to side with Prem Cheapda. My relatives started calling me every day which was something they had never done even when my mother was alive or dead.

Eventually, they decided they would threaten me and it was very filmy when they said, 'You better grant the divorce or it won't be good for you.'

At first I was in a state of denial and disbelief and then I asked them, 'What are the consequences?' After a prolonged and perhaps thoughtful silence, they said, 'Um . . . we won't talk to you any more.' Before they could continue I burst out laughing and replied, 'Thanks! That is not a punishment but a reward!' They were stunned. That's the point I think they gave up on me. After all, what could they do? I didn't owe them anything and they had no hold on me.

I heard later that they were waiting for me to call them and ask for help. That's when they would set me right and teach me a lesson. They would regain their superiority and of course, I would also be indebted to them for life. They felt that I had this coming since I was too arrogant, my mother had spoilt me, and I was too successful and had no manners. I've heard a lot of reasons for a marriage breaking up but not having manners as a primary reason can only be propounded so ingeniously by relatives.

But my poor relatives just waited and waited and then waited some more for me to call them for help and I never did—not once. Since they were out of the loop, they started asking me indirectly about what was happening in the case. Desperation for gossip, thy name is relatives. At first I bristled in self-righteous indignation and refused to meet them. But after some time, I decided to play along and have some fun at their expense. One of my mother's sisters called and asked to meet me. I met her at a restaurant.

The whole incident played out like a scene from absurd theatre!

Relative: 'How are you?'

Me: 'Brilliant. An American company is hiring me.'

Relative annoyed, but with a plastic smile on her face, eagerly covering up her scowl:

'Oh that's nice. How much are you getting paid?'

Me: 'Umm . . . what's the conversion rate for dollars these days? I don't know the rupee amount, it's a dollar salary.'

Relative, mouth hanging open and I spot her skin going green with jealousy: 'But what is the amount.'

Me: 'Ha-ha! I don't know. How are you?'

Relative: 'So what else is happening?' I think what she meant was, 'I am hoping you are losing the case you bitch.'

All the while, she kept trying to look sympathetic even with the sprouting hair in the beard on the chin which were very visible.

Me: 'Maasi, I'm just a little busy as the salary is enough for me to redo the house which is being paid for by the office. I have workers coming in and out all day. I also have to shop for a new car—company paid! But I have to go now—see you soon!'

Relative, finally getting frustrated and coming to the point: 'What's happening with your case?'

Me: 'Oh! That! I've been so busy that I haven't had time to think about it. It's going well. I think I am winning and you know, I am getting an interim maintenance now.'

Relative: 'I am so happy for you. Maybe you should talk to your uncle—he has this new investment business.'

Me: 'Is it the gold coin in pyramid form he is selling?'

Relative: 'Beta, I don't know. He is so smart and I just look after the home.'

Me: 'Sure. I'll invest for sure but what about the money you owed my mother? It's been ten years now.'

Relative (turning red and looking like an overgrown beetroot and closing and shutting her mouth like a fish): 'Waiter, just get some pakoras here. Beta, I've got to go. Your uncle is waiting for me.'

Off she slithered out while I laughed uproariously and then laughed some more, I was glad I came. It was free entertainment for me. But the humour aside, I was hassled by them at every stage. This only got worse when they found out that I was getting my interim maintenance. They scrambled over each other to ingratiate themselves with me, as though I was going to give them the money. Perhaps they just wanted to be around someone who was getting a little richer (by the princely sum of twelve thousand rupees), as though that would rub off on them.

I just sat back and enjoyed the show. I quickly got over the hurt of having relatives like these and was wishing that I didn't have any at all. I witnessed human nature at its worst. People can be mean and small-minded. They can be capable of kicking a hungry dog or beggar and be superciliously superior about it. They would pull somebody down just because he was helpless or poor or both. It saddened me but their foolishness made me laugh. It was and still is pathetic.

I also felt that their behaviour reflected their lack of love for my mother. The show of love only lasted until such time as she was alive and didn't extend to her progeny. The funny part is that all of these people do listen to religious discourses, go to the temple and espouse good thoughts like they are the embodiments of kindness and goodness. And then perform absolutely the opposite actions. It was inexplicable. They don't even understand what they stand for, which is really—nothing.

They would pester me around the time of religious festivals and call me to make me feel even more divorced or separated than I already was. They called to offer help when I didn't want any, to invest money, to give them help, to lend them jewellery. One of them even decided to have a frank chat with the very unfrank and close-minded Paneer Boy. He proceeded to Paneer Boy to tell him how spoilt I was and worse, details about an ex-boyfriend. Of course, this boyfriend's name was mentioned in the petition.

My relatives badmouthed me and insinuated that I was having affairs galore while the divorce was going on. At this stage, if anyone offered to have an affair with me, I wouldn't want one, but if I did, it would be purely physical. Well, I can't say that all my relatives were this bad, they just showed wickedness of varying degrees. Some didn't initiate the pettiness but they did nothing to stop it and defend me either. So, as far as I'm concerned, they are the same.

When I went overseas to visit my sister, her husband decided to lecture me on the ills of divorce and criticized me non-stop throughout my trip. I responded with a poker face, while he was saying things like all divorcees are whores. He believed that a woman should stay with her husband, no matter what. I thought at that point that if he was my husband, I would have probably started with a carving knife on his sanctimonious tongue and then proceeded to his private parts, à la the movie *Provoked*. But he was just another in the long line of 'well-meaning relatives' who didn't understand me or my situation and only felt that he could sanctimoniously lecture me.

What did I feel and wish for my relatives? At first, I wished them so much ill, but then, I pitied them because they were so stupid, they wouldn't know good luck even if it kissed them. I wished that they would not pass on the mind-set to the next generation and I would be able to get along with my cousins. But it was too late for that, because apples don't fall very far from trees and my cousins have all inherited the same attitude—they are like clones of their boorish mothers and spineless fathers.

I wonder what makes relatives bad friends. Perhaps it is the competitiveness and the feeling of oneupmanship. Maybe as they grow older they resent you for all the good things in your life, things that they never had, maybe they resent your youth and maybe they want to be you.

$$\star\star\star$$

'I am fasting for my husband's long life so that he can pay me alimony.' It was not exactly a typical response from an Indian housewife but it was the truth as I perceived it. Let me explain.

During my divorce, the pressure and pettiness from my relatives was much worse at festival times, especially during

Karva Chauth, when most Punjabi wives suddenly find a lot more love for their husbands than usual. Everyone was fasting and I didn't know what to do initially. At first there was shame at being married and not fasting. For the first couple of years, I braced myself and just went about my business and fasted. I then realized that I didn't care whether Paneer Boy was dead or alive. There was no point in killing myself fasting for him just to avoid questions.

After all, I was in no man's land as far as wifely duties were concerned. I was an illegal alien in marriage country so I decided to make up the rules as I went along and I'd deal with the consequences later. So I said no more of this deal with bullshit. As for my ever-present relatives, I gave them all kinds of distorted, ridiculous answers, mostly to rile them and to get a reaction out of them.

Diwali is another source of pressure and irritation. You can participate as a major player if you are the Lakshmi of the house as long as you are married. But if you are not then you become a pariah. So when my relatives started excluding me from the prayers and ceremonies, I started having the ceremony at my own home and brought street children into my celebrations. They also had no one and in some way were like me—abandoned by all and living only on Her Grace.

I just had to be positive in my thoughts, a bit thick-skinned and definitely wear my body suit to survive or relatives will kill you. In fact, for the couple of Diwalis I wasn't invited to my relatives' homes where I had been going to for years, it cut me up that I was snubbed so badly. However, I wasn't going to mope and cry and found my own methods to be happy at festive times. When they finally invited me back, I refused to go saying that I have a special Diwali planned with a group of street children. They couldn't believe it! But it was true—it was a special Diwali with all of us orphans together.

The Ganapati festival which is celebrated with pomp and show in Mumbai brought another rude surprise for me. I was invited to a cousin's house and just as the pooja was to start, one of my many maasis decided to be nasty yet again. In front of all the guests, she said that I shouldn't be there for the *aarti* ritual as I would bring bad luck to the proceedings. This wasn't her house and she was also a guest but she felt compelled to comment.

However, my cousin's wife said, 'She's always welcome here and she's done no wrong.' This was quite a revelation for me because it gave me assurance that all my relatives were not the same. Meanwhile, my maasi who was feeling a bit vanquished and sad that things didn't go according to her plan, proceeded to insult me by saying that I should answer an advertisement in the newspaper where some guy was looking for a woman and was willing to pay for it. I couldn't believe that she'd said such a thing. I asked her if she remembered what family I came from and the one that I had married into because if she weren't related to me, I wouldn't even be speaking with her. I couldn't believe that she'd got such an idea into her head. She couldn't be angrier that I had had the audacity to stand up for myself and muttered something about respect. I told her then that she'd need to give respect to get it back.

With all that was going on in my life, something finally had to give. For me, that incident was the absolute bottom of the barrel and no one bothered me after that. So if you are assertive and stand up for yourself, people treat you with respect. But if you don't speak up, they will trample all over you. But that's just life, I suppose.

I stopped wearing my mangal sutra because I'd sold it to survive, and I began to wonder whether my husband was my protector or destroyer, or indeed, nothing to me. The mangal sutra, the mark of a married woman, was as meaningless to me as the fake ones worn by the *bahu*s on television. I even stopped wearing sindoor. After all, why proclaim to the world that you are married when in effect you are fighting a bitter battle against your spouse? His actions, whether of his own volition or instigated by my father-in-law, seemed so cruel and unnecessary that I wished they would just let go and stop this trauma for me—and I am sure, for them as well. No one asked me about the absence of my mangal sutra or missing signs of matrimony. I think deep inside I started believing that despite all the religious and social trappings, I was definitely feeling, acting and behaving like an unmarried woman.

Was it tough? Sure but then who said dealing with social pressure would be easy? As I came to realize, it's not the process of divorce that's traumatic but all the drama and the three-ringed circus that goes with it. It is the comments, the barbs, the allegations and the stigma that cause the pain. Of course it is painful to lose your spouse and have your marriage break up. But the pain is exacerbated by all these unnecessary things and it's really like putting Zandu balm instead of Vaseline on a burn. Why do these people do it? I guess they are mean to start with and they can't digest anyone's happiness because they feel so deprived in all things in their life that they just need to vent their negativity on others.

I think once you are ready to accept the truth that your marriage is over, everything falls into place and then it doesn't seem so bad. It is still tough but at least you have this truth so it is only going to get better. When people ask me how to deal with their divorce, I share these experiences with them and ask them to try it. All my answers are from my personal experience. Are there any right or wrong answers? No, not really. You should learn from others' experiences as long as they are positive. As for the rest, don't forget the body suit of bravery because your mind, body and soul, and of course that elusive notion of character, *wohi character joh sirf ladki ka khaaraab hota hain* (only a girl's character is questioned), right from the time of Sita till us, the new age Sitas and Draupadis, is going to be attacked by the selfish and the petty-minded.

16

Kamasutra

Fat, grotesque woman 1 (W1): 'Let's not invite her. She's going through a divorce and will definitely be a bitch on heat.'

Skinny, dumb, wannabe woman 2 (W2): 'Yeah and I honestly think she is looking better with the weight she's lost since her divorce started.'

W1: 'And I have gained weight and just don't want to risk my husband around her.'

W2 (not taking the cue and saying the right things to her friend): 'Yeah, I know.'

W1: 'Go ahead and say it. You know, my husband has always liked her or rather, has lusted after her and will definitely go for her. And since she is going through a divorce, she is shameless. She will pounce on him like a hungry child left in a candy store.'

W2: 'You know, she looks like a damsel in distress now.' (This woman didn't know the rules of bitchiness at all!)

W1: 'No, it's just an act to get to the men.'

W2: 'But I didn't know she had a bad character.'

W1: (losing her patience): Now don't be so bloody dumb. Once you are married and your husband leaves you, you are like a half-eaten packet of chocolates. You can't be returned to the store, and well, someone is going to come after you since you are available. In short you are neither a virgin nor married so you are *public ka maal* [public property].'

W2: 'But why did you invite Surendra then? He is also going through a divorce, right?'

W1: 'Arre, he's a man, he's rich and there are different rules for men. They are always welcome especially since when you are marrying a divorced man, you focus more on his financial status—the stigma is less. A man never grows old and that applies to everything. Even if he has kids but is rich, it is the woman's job to look after the kids. It's so much easier for a man to get resettled than a woman. I hope we are clear now. No more invitations to you-know-who. In the meantime, I really must lose weight. I am almost 32 now—can't really risk a divorce!'

I was sitting on the next table, at a restaurant, separated by a pillar from these two women, who didn't even know me so well and were discussing my life. It was a painful way to know the truths of going through a divorce and see how society actually perceived me. The sexual overtones in a divorce are so weird, especially for a woman. There is sex and talk of sex everywhere. But the question that needs to be asked is where the actual action is. Is there any actual action or is it like a middle-aged drunk man who can't even get it up but boasts to his friends of his all-night power?

The gossip and the stories would make you think that women going through divorces are crazed nymphomaniacs. At divorce hearings they are so turned on by the interiors and exteriors of the court, the allegations of infidelity, abusive behaviour and the abysmal state of their life and finances, that they are literally stripping on the way back and jump into bed the minute they are home or perhaps even in the car, or worse still, auto, back from the court. Don't you think that it is both foolish and impossible? Then why are we so quick to pass judgements on women's characters when they are in a situation like this?

Why don't we consider that when a woman's life is in a shambles, the last thing in the world that she would like is to go to bed with someone? For heaven's sake, when you are just at the beginning of your divorce you are grappling with the dramatic change in your life's circumstances and feel like an acrobat swinging from a trapeze while balancing a life-changing act—divorce. Who really would even think of flirting, let alone sex? The law though doesn't have any provision for having sex with anyone when your case is going on. In fact, your lawyer will caution you to keep a low profile and avoid going out with or be seen having dinner or a rendezvous with men alone. So where is the question of wild sex as the gossips would have you believe?

In my case, looking at the state of my finances, relatives, and the gruelling grind of courts, I was so repulsed by the brutalities of life that the divorce was putting me through, that even the thought of flirting with any guy (except the family court peon for a date for the next hearing) was not on my radar. Any physical contact with the opposite sex was unthinkable. It was a marvel that I didn't develop any kind of hatred for men. Society does pass judgements on women but if they were to analyse the situation carefully, they would realize the ridiculousness and the implausibility of these baseless and hurtful statements

I think the real reason behind these brutal attacks on a woman's character and endless speculation about her sex life, besides a patriarchal mind-set of course, is human nature's penchant for gossip and the baser things in life. Another reason for the gossip is definitely the idea of the person being taught a lesson. I knew my relatives had propounded this reason to anyone and everyone who would listen. Of course, attacking the character of a woman has to be an integral part of maligning her—our oldest example is in the Ramayana when Ram put Sita through a trial by fire because of the words of a washerman. Not much has changed unfortunately, and even now we women are subject to trials by modern-day fires and we suffer, but fortunately, not in silence.

It's not just the women but even men have a different agenda. I remember suddenly becoming even more attractive to my friends' husbands. They wanted to offer me seedy liaisons under the guise of advice. They wanted me to be their business partners, and take these trips with them to conduct a recce for business. These offers weren't on the table when I was still living with my husband. One old geezer who was maybe even older than my father, had he been alive, insisted on giving me advice on the stock market on weekends at his farmhouse near Matheran. When I suggested talking about it in Mumbai, he refused saying that he would be able to explain it best at his farmhouse. I knew what he had in mind and it wasn't the intricate workings of the Indian stock market. I must admit, I did take tips from him very smartly. I roped in his wife and she became a conduit between us and she never ever suspected anything because there was really nothing to suspect.

I wanted to ask the old stock broker geezer why he didn't want to set me up with his sons who were my age and wanted me as a bed partner instead. Oh no, that thought would be blasphemous since I was used goods. When I asked them their reasons for this, this man turned around and said that his sons weren't as experienced as me and after all, what would the world say? Even here society is definitely biased towards divorced women and offers no respite. The relentless and ruthless persecution and categorization of women is unfair and continues unabated.

Another proposition that I got (and I swear I could've done with the change), but propriety prevailed and I didn't go, was when I was offered a trip to the Swiss Alps, all expenses paid, business-class travel and a five-star stay. The break would've done me good but what were the trade-offs? 'Sometimes, I tell you, even having a good character is an impediment,' I would joke to myself.

Something that these propositions made me realize, in an ironic way, was that at least if I had to settle down again and look for another relationship, I would definitely find it easier because hey, so many men found me desirable! The horrible truth of the matter is that none of these men had any honest helpful ways to actually get me out of this hole.

When I delved into the reasons for this 'divorce-specific sexual propositions', I realized that it was like my seal is broken so it's a case of used goods or rather second-hand goods for which you pay much lesser than the market rate of used goods.

This is no middle-class mentality, it cuts across like a knife through butter, across all the barriers of age and class and pervades through the spectrum. It's the woman who is cut off from the spectrum; she loses her friends as she has spent most of the time trying to fit in into the mould of the wife and focused more to get along with his friends.

It's like a red-carpet event 'for married couples only' and since she has broken the barriers, and is going through a divorce, she has now landed herself outside the ropes of the VIP barrier of society of married couples. Also, it's easier to criticize the woman because she is a softer target, because she often lacks societal support. We've being doing this for centuries, even a dhobi did it to Sita, and look where she landed up—in a jungle! You will be ostracized and land up in societal wilderness, condemned to live alone, fend for yourself and then shrivel up and die.

All this not only angered me but also hurt me deeply.

There is a fog that shrouds the sexuality of the woman in no man's land—divorce. What is really offensive is the 'nudge, nudge, wink, wink' response coupled with a slimy smile that characterizes the entire core of the sexuality of a woman in any event which is magnified more in such a situation. The surprising fact is that only women are subjected to these lewd propositions and I am sure they could make a living out of this if they wanted. No men are ever propositioned.

So only divorced women are ostracized for an apparent lack of character, labelled as sluts and sexual predators and are constantly propositioned—nothing even remotely similar happens to the men. The stigma for women is also unreasonably higher, especially for women with children— it's like you have sprouted another head or maybe there is a breast growing on your back, in short an abnormality. Since the differences in standards are harsher for women, I am glad that at least women have recourse to law.

But did I not have any sex at all till such time that the case was going on?

Well, initially because of the grind of the divorce, I didn't even think about it. This continued for a while and I did not even feel its absence. In fact, it was a relief because my spouse was no great shakes. Plus with the total occupation of all my senses with the court case, where was the time to miss sex? But after 4–6 years I started missing the physical intimacy and it was that phase of my life when most of my friends were married and some even had babies. There was a lot of physicality going around. There were times that I would give all the money in the world for physical intimacy but I could not do it.

Will someone please get up and change this system? During a divorce case in India, it is illegal to have sex with anyone. Worse still, if you have sex with your spouse, your divorce petition can be dismissed in court. In other words, NO SEX—if you have a divorce case going on.

Perhaps, the courts could work out a system where if your divorce is going on for more than a few years, you could then look at finding yourself another partner. That should work and the court should not perceive it badly. This needs to change because people who are in my predicament know what it really feels like. What can you do without destroying your case? What does one do when you are in a situation when you are allowed to have sex but it's with someone who you can't have it with—your spouse that you are divorcing? And that too is legally not permissible as mentioned earlier. All I can say is that the law is unfair and there should be some respite when your case seems to be running into many years. How long will you continue to be faithful to a husband on paper? We really aren't living in the same dark ages when these laws were formulated.

My case had been going on for six years and those were some of the most sexually alive years of my life. But the system did not allow me to seek intimacy because the repercussions were loss of face, money, character. The list is endless for losses and does not exist for gains.

So how did I beat the system? I invested in ways to pleasure myself. Am I embarrassed to say it? No, I am saddened and ashamed to be a part of the system that encourages such hypocrisy and brands anyone who is an adult and wants to have sex as a whore. I was dependent on the Kamasutra and myself for sexual satisfaction in the early stages of my divorce. But if you really want to know if I did or didn't have sex whilst going through my divorce, my honest response, clutching my injured heart would be 'nudge, nudge, wink, wink' and I am sure my broken heart would also nod mischievously and go 'nudge, nudge, wink, wink'.

17

Shatter Shatter

What is that lying on the road? It looks like a clump of red, very small in size but it seems flattened out. Wait, it seems to have shattered into smithereens. The lump has a line of red which seems to be still running, like a rivulet. The line, the clump and the lump is my broken and bleeding heart.

Does one become immune to daggers and pistols aimed at your heart in the divorce petition, by your spouse, just because on paper you are supposed to be apart? Ah, if words dictated everything then I'm sure writers would be the most powerful, resolute, strong-willed people in the world. Alas! Though words have a great capacity to hurt, yet whatever we write doesn't always translate into action. Paneer Boy and I were to be now parted and we had done all those horrible things to each other, so illustrated and exaggerated in the petition. Yet why was I so disheartened by the changed status?

I only knew that I had spent so many private moments with this person. In fact, the most intimate ones, almost bordering on being illicit, are like when you are getting ready to go to bed. You know that in the initial stages of your marriage, going to bed is a euphemism for making love. I knew that when I went into the bedroom we would be together. I wore my sexiest nightie or peignoir. I even wore some perfume to smell divine and maybe feel like Marilyn Monroe who famously said, 'I wear only Chanel No 5 to bed.'

Then I'd pretend to read with the lights on but was actually waiting for him to come to the room. Then when he came in, I knew the night had actually started. He would come to the bed wearing a kurta pyjama and also smelling of a citrusy aftershave, and make some small talk. This would feel like waiting at a red signal, waiting for the lights to turn green so that we could go ahead. Then he would hold my hand and talk some more. Then his hand would wander all over my body. We would kiss passionately, which both of us knew was the precursor of more intimate actions.

After sharing such closeness, what compels a person to spill their guts in a divorce petition which would be read by strangers, the lawyers, and then the judges? What is even more hurtful is that they are professionals and do it as a duty and frankly don't even give a damn. After you marry, you are meant to be one with your spouse but none of this comes into his mind when he is filing a petition and littering it with so many cruel and insensitive truths and untruths. It's like you are nude and have been splatted across the page like a fly swatted against a dirty yellow paper. This seems like yellow journalism, but no one pays to buy or read this news. In fact, you have to pay the lawyers for wanting to read this news, 'YOU ARE GETTING DIVORCED.'

I do not understand the compulsion to share our private lives. I did it because I had to respond to the allegations levelled at me. But I did not understand his need to do this. If he had thought of our bodies wrapped around each other or the intimacy of the afterglow, he might have been kinder on paper. Or maybe I was wrong. Maybe our lovemaking for him was just fucking without much meaning. I do not see how after so much love, there can be so much viciousness and hatred.

When there were good times, like celebrating our birthdays, the joy in the room could light up the world. It was unbelievable, the surprise and excitement of giving each other gifts and then dressing up and going out together for a meal. It was brilliant. The memory of these good times together made my heart ache even more. I felt like a piece of me, the one that had believed in happily ever after with Prince Charming, had been tossed out of the window like yesterday's newspaper. Or worse still, it had been used to wrap fish and the fish was like my life—stinky and dead.

My heartbreak really did lead me to lose faith in being in love and being with another man for quite some time. I can't say that I became a cynic but stopped being a believer for a while because I couldn't subject my heart to the investment of being in a relationship. While I was still quite low and depressed, I stopped questioning the cause of my divorce and asking myself why Paneer Boy had done this to me. But at least I am sure my lawyer was happy with the way I looked in court—a full-blown tragedy queen who would definitely arouse the judge's sympathy.

I think feeling conned and used and as a result humiliated helps you get over the heartbreak. I felt that I had loved Paneer Boy and he hadn't loved me. I felt let down because I felt I was someone special and just couldn't believe that he had treated me like this. At some point, I also began to get the feeling that he must have felt that he was better than me and hence left me. My humiliation led to anger and finally to wanting to avenge myself. I entered a vicious cycle of enhancing my heartbreak. You want to get over the embarrassment of being left high and dry. Your ego has been hurt and seeks punishment for the one who has committed this crime.

I guess I sought retribution for my heartbreak and retaliated by wearing my body suit of prayers tighter. I also started going out with the opposite sex to prove to myself that I wasn't unattractive. I couldn't tell this to my husband since the case was going on. But it was as though I wanted to prove to him, 'Look, what you have missed out on.' It was a childish way of retaliation, but heartbreak does that to you and we all get afflicted by the rebound syndrome. I must admit that I got my affirmation from the other guys and it felt like just what the doctor had ordered. The childish, harmless flirtations boosted my suffering self-esteem and took it higher.

You, and I am sure everyone in the divorce predicament,

also feel betrayed because it is like the last bastion of your privacy has fallen and anyone can do anything to you. I felt that if someone I had shared my wedding vows with could do this to me, then there is no one in the world that I could trust. Somehow, seeing the petition in black and white further enhances the finality of your situation. It's the documentation of your heartbreak that is wrenching your heart out of your body. Betrayal hurts and you feel let down and don't know who to trust and who not to. The next time round, be it in love or maybe another marriage, you proceed with caution. I resorted to eating out a lot and pretty much living on chocolate to bail me out. I ate to feel better. The comfort food took away my pain temporarily. But when I got onto the weighing scale, the pain turned into shock especially seeing the rising figures of my weight!

But I know I wasn't bitter because that only burns you up inside like acid on your body, chewing up your flesh. I knew I had been unfortunate in my life but I did not want that be the yardstick of future relationships. I believe in happy endings. So what if one ending was not happy, maybe this was God's plan of avoiding a bigger unhappiness. I learned to see not only the trees but also the forest. So maybe this time my heart had gone kaput for a reason. Maybe if I had stayed on longer in the relationship not only my heart but even other parts of me would have gone kaput. Pessimism and bitterness are not the answer but looking towards a brighter horizon is because no one wants emotional baggage as it packs in countless pounds on your psyche. Physical weight you can get rid of by working out, but there is no readily available remedy for weighty emotional baggage with which I am sure if I dared to get on to a weighing scale it would C-R-A-C-K under both the weights—emotional and physical.

18

200 Pounds and Counting

Creak, ugh, C–R–E–A–K, Aiyah, aaah, aaah, grunt, u–f–f f! Oh, no! Not again! Get off me, I can't take this any more! Get off me! Do u hear me? Do you want to kill me? These are the words I am confident that my weighing scale was screaming at me. I am sure that if I could ask my weight to get off me I would've said the same thing. Unfortunately, I wasn't the weighing scale and had to put up with the extra tonnage.

My weighing scale wasn't bothered by inflation and stuck it out resolutely in the 90s. Only a couple of times it got any lower but those were mere blips in the graph of my weight loss saga. The fat cells were now there to stay and had, in fact, made themselves very comfortable in my roomy body. After all this was Mumbai and instead of staying in a flat—a thin person's body—they were staying in a spacious bungalow—my roomy body. My weight was like Sachin's centuries—it kept on getting higher and soon it had reached the triple digit finish line which was something that I thought only happened to middle-aged housewives, not to someone like me. This couldn't be happening to me. Yes, in plain words, I had become fat.

I had no choice but to deal with it, so the tough part had just started. I had no idea how it felt to be fat. In school, I had played basketball and table tennis. I was an athlete and competed in the shot-put events. All these required a high degree of fitness so there was never any question of being tubby. Besides, I also walked and cycled about 10 km a day since I lived on a farm and was surrounded by 15 acres of vegetation. It was as healthy a life as could be. I was always a big girl in terms of height—5 feet 8 inches—and was well built and not puny or delicate, but weight was never a serious issue. It could also never be since we grew up in a farm and ate all fresh food, poultry and never any processed food, as it was not only considered unhealthy but was infinitely more expensive than eating home-grown food. My dad was an Olympic level cyclist so the insistence on eating healthy food and also exercising was foremost. So I had never been fat all my life and in fact had maintained a healthy weight for most of my childhood.

However, all this changed once my case started. Even though I found little or no time to exercise, my appetite remained the same. I found a complete disconnect between my brain and my hand reaching out to get the chocolate chip cookies. No one told it to stop. Actually I am lying, even to myself, I think everyone finds the time to exercise if they are motivated enough, but I just wasn't. I felt tired and lethargic and frankly did not give a damn about what I ate or how my body looked. Maybe it was my depression that caused me to think and behave like that.

And sure enough, one of the manifestations of depression is not looking after yourself physically. The divorce which seemed endless and entangled like Medusa's hair had definitely left me depressed and that in turn impacted my health. My body faced the ravages of that. I was fat and huge. It just made me feel uncomfortable and unable to face up to the challenge of it. How does one deal with being fat if all your life you have not been fat? Being fat was a new experience for me, an experience I did not like.

My self-esteem did not suffer at all. Maybe if it had I would've done something about weight loss, but the number of men still throwing themselves at me ensured that I had a good body image. Because, although I would like to be fit as I was before, yet in my mind I was defined by more than just my physical appearance.

Everyone of course felt the need to continue lecturing me about my weight. In India they think nothing of calling you fat. In fact, when you meet someone after a while, it is pretty much the first thing they will tell you. They will then inundate you with information about miracle weight loss diets, a cabbage soup diet, a soup diet, pumpkin seeds diet, no carbs, no protein, and tell you about the dietician who's a magician and can dissolve the fats from places you didn't even know fat existed, like the mole in your underarms. I listened politely and then at times wanted to say, 'Go to hell! I've got bigger things on my mind; I've got a divorce going on and no one to help me. I couldn't care less if look like a beached whale—I just want my divorce case to be over. If you can't help or empathize with me at least stop discussing only my weight while my life is on hold.' But I said nothing and covered up my hurt with humour because I didn't have a choice.

Discussing weight is like a national pastime in India and it's not like the people discussing it are the very epitome of fitness. In fact, they just seem to dispense advice as they suck in their stomachs and hope that you will compliment them on their weight loss.

Even though I ignored the barbs and blatant references to my weight I felt other aspects of weight gain more acutely. My body ached with the excessive weight. My knees were definitely making sounds like Beethoven's orchestra gone wrong. My back felt like it had pins and needles stuck in it. And I had to constantly apply all sorts of creams to ease the pain. So my body at this young age had become an assortment of pains and aches and felt like a tin man screwed together by nuts and bolts which could come unscrewed at any time and cause me to double over in pain. During the course of a decade, the length of my divorce case, I was laid up in bed about six times, unable to move because of the pain caused due to being overweight.

Then why didn't I lose weight? I did try. At first I joined the gym. In fact, after the first year of languishing in court and my second Diwali when no one had invited me over for the pooja, I was the only one working out embarrassingly alone in the Khar Gymkhana gymnasium. I used to work out religiously for two hours a day and had even lost about 30 kg. I looked and felt good. But the thin phase did not last long because I soon got a bad order in court and again started eating and started making excuses for not exercising.

Before long the clothes that I had bought in my thinner days became a tad tight and then the jeans, which are always a reliable indicator of weight, started protesting each time I got into them. When I went on to the next size, I felt a little relieved. Of course, I didn't throw away my old jeans—I stored them away, vowing to fit into them soon. At the next size again the same pattern repeated itself and before I knew it, I had already reached the next size. In fact, there were so many next sizes that I lost count. If India's GDP had grown at the same rate as my weight, we would have beaten any country in the world and would've been on the superhighway to success. This pattern of weight loss and gain depending upon a judgement became a regular recurrent pattern of my life.

I realized that I was an emotional eater and each time anything significant happened, I would eat. Besides, having no family added to the stress. The divorce proceedings had definitely changed my life yet again. I never knew that I, who was an athlete, could be like this. This goes to show that divorce can bring about so many insidious changes in our lives. It is like a poisonous gas, which at first is unnoticeable but then pervades our whole being and we must know what to do, when to stop and when to get out. This is because it is principally the two parties/people involved who suffer the maximum as all the others only inherit second-hand burns.

I know so many women going through divorce who not only have suffered myriad health problems but have also ended up going for counselling and even psychiatric treatment. So many simply pretend, like I did initially, that they are not divorced and that their husband is out of town. In fact, their pretence continues for a lifetime. And, these are educated working women—one of them is in fact a marriage counsellor herself, if you can believe! To heal yourself, you must first be honest with yourself, as you can't help others cope if you base your life on a foundation of lies.

My weight yo-yoing became a constant source of concern for me and also a source of amusement to my friends. On the bright side, at least I had clothes in all sizes since I was optimistic and would keep the earlier clothes in the hope that I would fit back in them and I also did fit back into them more than once. I just kept on gaining and losing weight, just like the stock market gaining and losing points.

I even started following all sorts of fad diets. So one day it was an idli diet, then the General Motors diet, then the watermelon diet, then the cabbage soup diet, then an all-salads diet, it was endless. I would succeed for a few days and then get back to binge eating. As a result, I gained more weight than I had lost and for the first time in my life I felt my willpower faltering and I felt that there is something that I can't conquer and vanquish. I wish I had spent the time on eating right and exercising right. I guess all that I had learnt in my childhood had come to a nought in these times. In a span of a decade, I lost and gained about 400–500 kg. I guess my genes must be really strong or else I would definitely have been writing this posthumously.

I only thank God that I didn't have to seriously date anyone at this time since on paper I was married. It would be impossible to be romantic with anyone. I definitely had no inclination towards sex as my body felt so grotesque. Being in a serious relationship with anyone was out of the question. For the first time in my life I was happy to be going through a divorce.

I asked myself if I learned anything from being fat. I can say that I learnt that it is important to value your body and not let external factors harm it. I know that nothing in this world is worth losing your health over. I learnt that it is damn difficult to lose weight. I always joke and say that losing weight is like making money honestly in India—damn difficult but not impossible. I learnt that divorce, even unknowingly, impacts every aspect of your life and when you think you are in charge you may actually be cruising out of control. Do I blame the divorce? No, I have never blamed my divorce for anything bad that has happened in my life; on the contrary, I say that it is a learning experience. When you find something else to blame your problems on, it is just convenience and you never change, as you only find a peg to hang your coat on which takes you away from the truth. It doesn't help you to focus inwards and question where you are lacking but just lets you find an easy scapegoat. I may have my faults but not learning from my mistakes is definitely not one of them.

I reluctantly boarded the roller coaster of yo-yoing weight loss and gain. The emotional highs and lows that came with it also unleashed their own damage to my physical, mental and emotional well-being. But I still haven't given up on weight loss. Despite being weak in mathematics all my life, I have learnt the number crunching of calories to my varying vital statistics of 40–36–44 to 38–32–40 to 36–30–39 to 40–35–43 to 39–34–38 to infinity to hopefully my desired statistics of 38–24–36.

19

Prozac

Darkness . . . despair . . . destruction . . . these were the thoughts in my mind when the case was going on and it seemed endless. Why was it happening to me? Did I do anything wrong in this life or my past life? It is funny how during these times you always turn to the other beliefs to help you get through this. I felt all I did was go from one court date to another. My ritual remained the same, take an auto, go to court, pray in that makeshift temple, climb the stairs, grab a seat, keep my bag there to reserve it, look for my number on the roll call, come back, put on my iPod, read the paper and wait . . . endlessly.

Desolation, despondency—these feelings characterized my actions during these times which are difficult to describe. I just looked for an outlet, which was not forthcoming, to escape and all entertainments seemed so transient, the only permanence seemed to be the damn case which was not moving and was in my life and seemed like the file in a babu's hand which had gone into the black hole of babudom. So many questions tormented me and yet I knew that those were questions that had no real answer, something like a child asking whether the moon was made of cheese or if there was a man in the moon.

Devastation . . . difficult . . . defiled . . . is how my mind and body felt. The irony is that one day you are married and the next you are in court hashing each other's sex lives or absence of it. Of course, you are portrayed as the woman who can't get enough of men or sex but not with your husband and you do nothing throughout the day but make plans to spend his money on yourself, don't look after the house and spend the time tumbling in and out of other men's beds instead. If I had a rupee for every man they said I had slept with, I'd be richer than Bill Gates.

Donkey . . . douche bag . . . dumb is what I was for not taking off with at least some of their money. I didn't even have enough of their jewellery. Hey! In my world, we trusted everyone and they were at some point my friends. How was I to know better? I should've been like a typical money grabbing character and just done a number on them. But then my so called goodness came to the fore and I just didn't do anything and here I was, practically starving. But hey, I am a good, kind soul, and that got to count for something.

Destitute . . . desperate . . . drowning in sorrow were also ways to describe me. I knew I had to pick myself up or they would win. It was true that it was the mother of all battles but I couldn't let down my parents without putting up a fight. I just couldn't lie back and expect to be rescued. My relatives would of course trample me and take all my money or whatever I was left with and definitely rejoice that I had gone. 'Don't ask' had become my mantra to all the invasive, inane, hurtful, unnecessary, vicious questions asked by my 'lovable' relatives about my divorce case.

Death . . . depression . . . divorce. These three disastrously morbid words that go hand in hand were 'me' at that time. At the beginning of the case, my concentration was lacking, my ability to work bordered on zero if not negative and my desire to live—at complete rock bottom. I couldn't understand why I felt this way. I'm actually glad that it is difficult to get a gun in India otherwise I shudder to think what I would have done—to myself or someone else, I don't know.

I had always excelled at everything and living through this experience completely shattered me. I felt I was an absolute failure and I felt it was entirely my fault. No one told me that what I was going through had shared blame and both parties were contributors. In my diminished state of mind, I didn't realize that I was punishing myself and judging myself too harshly and I should not have been doing that. In fact, I should have definitely been going easy on myself and excusing whatever misdemeanours I may have committed. But no. That was the time I decided to subject myself to microscopic examination and put my soul through a sugarcane crusher. I kept on doing this to myself till I had no juice left in me to come out. If there were any remnants, I ran those through both a mixer grinder and a hand grinder, pounding away at myself. But the good part of this is that I reached the bottom of the bottomless pit, and finally while lying there, at an abysmal low, I started thinking differently.

I knew I had in me a fighting spirit, a survivor's uncanny sixth sense, almost Gloria Gaynor-esque in my glory. I just had to find that strength. I had lost my mojo and had to get it or grab it back. So I decided that step by step I would get it back. I was on the brink but I hadn't yet gone over. I was already naked and had nothing to lose so all I could do was dust myself and pick myself up. And that's exactly what I did.

And when I did, life started to perk up. It's like I got a plastic surgery done of the crap in my life and got a new life—being all fixed so that no sorrowful expression crossed my mind or showed on my face. Slowly but surely, combined with good food, exercise, walks, friends, avoiding pests (my relatives), meditation, going to the club, reading and being inspired by iconic people like Shobhaa Dé, Gloria Steinem and Oprah Winfrey, my mind underwent that metaphorical plastic surgery. I had become a master juggler with my emotional state and worked very hard to keep the darkness at bay.

But I was still hiding behind a façade of dark lies at my workplace. I was sure that I would take care of it soon, because if I had made it this far in the obstacle race of divorce, I would also be able to jump over the obstacles at my workplace.

And yet, sometimes, when I am by myself and the workplace does not provide the solace and comfort of just being with human beings, I would wonder how tender the nerves in my wrist are . . . and the blood around them . . . my white wrists turning blood red . . . and the life seeping away from my body . . . demonic and destructive.

20

Employee/Billa No: 786

Was my nose longer than Pinocchio? Maybe it was, I'm not sure. If you tell a lie, your nose becomes longer is what you had been told as a child and I wondered if it was true as an adult. If it did, then I was in trouble.

I was definitely lying through my teeth at work when anyone asked me about my marital status. During my divorce, at all organizations I had worked at, I said that I was married. The weird part is that I didn't have to lie. I am a truthful person and abhor lies and liars. All my friends tell me that I should sometimes lie to save a situation. They also say that it is the strictness with which I always tell the truth that gets me into trouble.

Then why did I lie and keep on promoting an embellished version of the truth? I just didn't feel like facing up to the challenges that came with telling the truth because it was too painful to explain what I was going through to them. The breakdown of a marriage is not a simple matter and if I did accept that my marriage was breaking down, there would have been questions which I just didn't want to answer. I also did not want to be whispered about, which usually happens in these cases. I had already suffered that first hand with my relatives and the thought of enduring it at work was enough to make me lie even more than a politician caught with his hand in the till.

I felt like a failure and had a number of related insecurities—I didn't want to share this with colleagues whom I barely knew. It's not like they were my friends and would take up cudgels on my behalf. A problem like this is really personal and you want to keep it private because you can't always explain the entire nuanced truth to people at work. Colleagues can sometimes also be judgemental and I did not want to be judged. I definitely did not want to be thought of as a failure. I keep reiterating failure because the usual way of seeing a divorce is as a failed marriage and hence, by extension a person undergoing divorce is also seen as a failure. And these estimations of our personal worth definitely matter a lot to us, especially in these bleak times. We are demolished by others' words and their yardsticks serve as a measure of our personal worth.

I often wondered and thought that the stigma of divorce is an exaggeration, that times have changed and nowadays, people just don't think that divorce is a big deal especially in the workplace, in a cosmopolitan city like Mumbai. Well, I was wrong. When I casually asked a colleague who was also going through divorce (funnily enough, we found out about each other's divorces because we bumped into each other accidentally at the family court), whether her team knew about it. She looked at me with horror and said, 'Are you mad?' She then looked around surreptitiously and whispered conspiratorially while pleadingly adding, 'Please don't tell them.'

This made me very curious and I casually surveyed a number of people in the office about whether they would disclose their divorced status to their colleagues. About 95 per cent of them answered with a resounding 'No'. The reasons varied—from not wanting to be a part of the stigma involved to their divorce not being any business of their colleagues as they kept their personal and professional lives apart. I also subscribed to these reasons for a long time but truth be told, it was just easier to lie than to tell the truth.

Besides, I felt that getting a divorce is like a black spot in your life and I don't mean like the dark spot in the moon which is supposed to enhance its beauty. This was a negative mark against your moral fibre and morality. At work, you want to appear as though you are Superwoman and hence, you just don't want this aberration to be brought forth. Until our society accepts divorce as a fact of life, people going through divorce will continue to spin Grimm's *Fairy Tales* of our blemished personal lives.

So I just made up incredible tales about why my husband never came to any get-togethers at work and never ever objected to my staying late at work. Worse still, I had to spin outrageous stories about why I wasn't having kids, which as we all know in India everyone feels that they have a right to know and offer an opinion on. After all, I had been married for around seven years so why wasn't I having children. I gave them reasons like we were still in the honeymoon phase of our marriage and proceeded to giggle like a giddy-headed teenager. I also tried hard to get a moony look in my eyes. I was cringing inside but it was less cumbersome to lie and conform to society's norms because there would be fewer questions. People accept you easily when you fall in the pattern of accepted behaviour. A divorcee is still considered an outsider in this system.

When I went to America on work and ended up needing to stay for almost six months, it really brought out the story teller in me to convince my colleagues that my husband was anxious to have me back and would fly out if I was to stay any longer. It was actually my lawyer who was demanding I get back because she was tired of making excuses to the judge who was hopping mad and taking out his anger on my lawyer. I also pretended to be calling my husband regularly when I was actually calling Bobby to check if all was well at home in my absence. It was all so complicated but it was still easier than telling the truth.

Additionally, if you also say that you are married there are fewer passes at you and the subtle dynamics of flirting at the workplace ensure that there are no lines crossed if both parties don't want to cross them. I kept the walls firmly in place and managed a pretty good work–life balance by drawing an iron curtain to separate life at work versus personal life.

I also managed to adjust my timings at work whenever I needed to appear in court. I would carry a change of clothes with me and sneak into the loo at the office to change into the widow-like outfit which was my standard court wear and vice versa. I didn't take any leave because it would be embarrassing to ask for leave for a court date and it would also expose the lie I had propounded of my happily married life. I would request to be allowed to come in late and would stay back late on these occasions. Since I was on top of things at work, no one really objected.

My general demeanour at office was to be and act, as normally as possible. I would work assiduously and even put in extra hours without complaining. I guess that is why they say that single people make better workers. I made a few friends at work but I was always a bit uneasy to ever get too close because one of my fundamental rules of friendship is that you can't base it on dishonesty.

Sometime around 2007, I participated in Lead India, a leadership initiative contest led by the *Times of India* which invited participants from all over India as prospective leaders. Since I made it to the top eight finalists in Mumbai, my photographs along with all my personal details which I had so far kept away from the office were splashed across the front page of *TOI*. You would have to have been living under a rock to not have read the truth about my marital status, and that too as the headlines. And so, the truth did filter into the office.

What came as a surprise, however, was the attitude of some of my colleagues. They were kind and invited me out to social gatherings with them. At first, I was a bit suspicious and thought they were trying to test me, but I didn't refuse the invitation. I think somewhere I also wanted to put an end to the façade. I went with them and to my great surprise, they were dignified and didn't once ask me about the divorce. They just chatted along normally.

Despite being pleasantly surprised, I was suspicious and waited to see if they'd bring it up the next time. But even then, nothing happened. These outings soon became routine and I actually started enjoying myself. These friends became like a new family for me. These were outings without judgement or advice—it was like I was unmarried again. My colleagues had become my 'going out friends'. I can't say that they were like my other friends, but at least we had gone beyond being just workmates and I can tell you that it felt good. In fact, I often wished that the truth had come out in the open earlier, then I could have probably made some more friends who could have been a pillar of strength during the tough times. Perhaps I wouldn't have to be creeping into the office loo to change out of my court outfit. Who knows, I could've taken some leave from my boss as well.

I am glad that I saw this aspect of people. It lessened the impact of those who refused to accept the changing face of society. The winds of change are sweeping through society and maybe thirty years down the line divorce will not be stigmatized and people like me will not be forced to use euphemisms for divorce, at least not at the workplace. We would be able get on with our daily lives which in itself is pretty exciting with so much going on—work, relatives, friends, divorce case, money, social gatherings to name a few—without interruption and stigma.

21

Dal Chawal and Some Mirchi

Tic, tic, tic . . . this was the monotony of court dates. It was like eating dal, rice everyday without respite, with never a vada pav in sight and there's no point in dreaming of pizza. What was going on? Did our legal system suck so much? Did we all have so much free time that we could spend whole days in court only to come back with the princely prize of . . . NOTHING! You'd maybe get a new court date after four months and then needed to fervently pray that the judge would not be on leave.

What you see in the movies or on television where there is immediate resolution of a crime with punishment swiftly following after is just a fantasy world. However, the horror stories you hear about two generations fighting in court are true. I shuddered to think of my fate. I yo-yoed from one court date to another and the court date became the walls separating each compartment of my life. Then I saw that each court date was the defining point of my life and everything else was in-between. Even then it seemed like a sad waste of a talented young woman.

Nothing ever changed. The courts were never painted, the clerks were transferred after two or three years, the judges also got transferred to other cities, and the lawyers were still demanding money and lording over the clients unless you were someone really important.

I always went to the little makeshift temple. It was just a foot-high deity lodged in a niche created on a tiled platform below a shady banyan tree just outside the court. There would be people behind me queuing up to also say their prayers and sometimes I would meet the same litigants on my floor in the court or who I had seen from time to time coming again and again to court. I would rush and finish in one minute, take my prasad and hope my prayers would yield the benefits. It's ironic we pray to God for a minute in this rushed buzz of the day and that too for a case that goes on forever. I would then get off on the right floor, and reserve a seat outside my courtroom where my case was going on by keeping my bag there. The courtroom also evoked a sense of ownership because, after all, I had been coming here for almost eight years now. I would then have my name checked on the roster and would sit staring into space and trying to avoid my fellow inmates because the family court was a mental and emotional jail.

I'd look at the news, read the gossip, listen to my iPod, eat a little and wait. It's the waiting that kills you and there is so much of it you do. Each date was like a drop of water waiting for freedom. It was like undergoing Chinese water torture because it is the waiting for the next drop that drives you crazy. You wait for a court date, your lawyer, the judge, the money, the spouse, the acceptance, love of people, and wait and wait for this hell to be over. Sometimes words cannot sufficiently describe the dreary atmosphere and the feeling of loss and listlessness in the family court.

My routine in the court remained exactly the same. When my lawyer would arrive, we would go inside the court and listen to some nonsense from the judge about settling the matter amicably. He would also talk about disposing some new minor petition in my matter which was a frivolous petition filed by my soon to be ex-husband's family to delay the proceedings. We would then present our answer, after which, they would counter it and so the whole interminable whirlpool continued to spin. Also, after this petition was dismissed, my lawyer and I then filed a frivolous petition asking for the inspection of some papers. Clearly, we weren't going to back off and stop filing frivolous petitions. The game of cat and mouse becomes catch me if you can. It is amazing how these petitions can delay a case for up to six months at a time— it gives you a real perspective about the sheer amount of time involved in divorce cases.

Both my soon to be ex-husband and I continued with these petitions for such a long time that by the time the main case came up for hearing, we each had about 2000 pages worth of petitions in our files, and they were all filled with junk. I could précis all of that in less than 100 words, maybe even twenty-five. Does anyone care about the system? Nope, each litigant, lawyer and every person in India who has had even a brief interaction directly or indirectly with the legal system has millions of excuses right from the ever increasing population to not having enough judges. But no one questions the system or tries to change it. If the law minister couldn't provide a principal for the Government Law College in Mumbai for a number of years, what hope do we have of changing this system?

What happens to us poor litigants in all this? It seems unfair that we come into the divorce courts as bright young people and leave as disgruntled and cynical adults having wasted, if we are lucky, fifteen years of our life here. The physical changes in our body from slim frames to thickened waists and wrinkled necks are obvious for all to see. These changes perhaps reflect the wizening of our souls as well. The mental changes are not visible but are far more devastating and far too numerous to enumerate but it's like surviving and learning to live again after a nuclear bomb. Can't we logistically streamline the process of divorce or use alternate dispute resolution methods like arbitration and make them binding on a couple? They may be simplistic solutions but perhaps there is collusion in the system to avoid resolving divorces so that the judges can justify their jobs, the lawyers can loot their clients, and the villains can just file one stay order and have the matter in court for years.

The litigant also wastes her time, money and peace of

mind in a fruitless exercise because sometimes when the judgement comes in, it's too late and all the time wasted doesn't make the entire process worth it. Of course, there is always the recourse to appeal the judgement which wastes even more time. The appeal can go to the High Court and then Supreme Court and finally the judgement comes in and you are happy . . . that's if you aren't dead, if not physically then in all other ways.

Another heart-wrenching fallout of the socio-legal system of divorce in India is the absence of communication between the two parties unless it is through the lawyers. You can't even be civil and say hello. The parties will, however, talk when there are accusations to be hurled. Every word is challenged in and out of court and each penny fought for and every insult traded and exchanged and all the drama. Everyone says 'my marriage was unhappy from day one' but I cannot understand why it takes people ten years and two kids to walk out.

But there are always a few poignantly humorous episodes in court, where a woman took out a bottle of poison in the courtroom and in filmy style flung it at the lawyer before the judge, cursed her husband and said, 'If you don't give me my money, I will kill myself.' The poison was fake but she made her point! Another woman came to court with her 'boyfriend' and it didn't go down well with the judge. It was weird and everyone both inside and outside the courtroom kept wondering as to why on earth would someone come with their boyfriend to a court where you are divorcing your husband. The brazenness of it added to the foolishness and desperation of it. Another time, a woman openly called her mother-in-law a slut and proceeded to tell her father-in-law about all the men his wife was involved with! The poor man promptly engaged the son's lawyer himself. There was another time that a clerk went on long leave and took up a job as a private detective to supply information about the cases to the respective parties. He never got caught though. It was all happening in the divorce courts. They were like an epic movie packed with the ingredients of love, sex, humour, action, villains, vamps, heroes, heroines, item girls and the extras. But the question remains—how had the court impacted me?

My appearance had gone from catwalk model to rat walk and it was when someone jeered at me, my looks and predicament and said some very cruel words, that I snapped out of my morbid reverie. It is a tragic state that the courts put you in and then because of the self-fulfilling prophecy you become a court rat. You live the life, dress bad, look bad, and feel bad and of course, bad things happen to you. But that cruel jeer saved me, like they say, you can always turn around a negative into a positive. I decided I wanted no part of this misery and was determined to live a life. I would not just be defined by the start and finish line of court dates for the rest my life. I would live well and not mope at all. Whatever I would do, I would love my life and that would for sure be the best that I could do for myself. Like they say, the best that you can do for yourself is live well because living well is the best revenge.

I cleaned up my entire appearance and also my mind-set and I felt as shiny as a new penny. It took me six months of friend therapy, avoiding relatives, my lawyer, skipping a few dates, and praying until I felt healed and ready to take on the world. I was ready to be churned out as a brightly minted coin. No one was going to stop me whether it was my relatives, my detractors or my in-laws.

22

Outlaws

Heroes, vamps, heroines, vamps, supporting actors, item girls.
The roles essayed by you as perceived by the in-laws, as the
case progresses.

Love, murderous rage, anger, concern, betrayal.
The emotions that your in-laws arouse, in you, as the case
progresses.

Usually, before a divorce matter comes to court, parents
from both sides try to get it resolved. They try everything
in the book to keep the marriage going. The usual remedies
are first offered—have a child, take a vacation, take a break
from each other for some time. Then come the emotional
entreaties—what will the world say; think about your
child; think about your reputation; what will you do ahead

because you will never ever be able to get someone else now that you are a divorcee. For the woman especially, there is much talk of how we will manage financially. If nothing works, then comes the final blow—think of our reputation, we will suffer a lot. In India, everyone is a stakeholder in the marriage and sometimes the parents have, let's say, the promoter's quota. Initially, the pleas for keeping the marriage going persist.

However, once it is clear that that there can be no reconciliation, the about-turn amazes you. They start with, 'Don't worry we will fight for you, you aren't alone;' 'He/she doesn't know what they are losing out on;' 'Their case is so weak, it will not stand a chance in court;' 'We treated him like a son or daughter and they have no gratitude or consideration. If I had brought up a dog it would've been better;' 'He/she thinks no end of themselves, and we should teach them a lesson in court;' 'You are blameless; it is all his/her fault;' 'Don't worry we will find a better guy/girl for you (like at that time all you are thinking of is resettling, sleeping with a jagged rock would be preferable).'

Bizarrely enough, there is also competition among those who get divorced and their ex-in-laws, about who will get married first and get a bigger, better deal. I once heard a cousin's ex-husband remarking that he would produce not only a kid but a boy to show her. When I wondered what was going on, I was told that the marriage had ended in divorce because of the husband's impotency and now the man wanted to prove her wrong and show her that the fault lay with her. But to have a child, be it a boy or a girl, her ex must be able to defy nature altogether. The last I heard of them was that they each remarried and had children, though I don't know the gender!

Prem Cheapda, of course, didn't want any kind of settlement because he felt I had erred and needed to be punished. He was God in his family so the rest of them toed the line. He is one of the people, along with my brother-in-law, that I hold responsible for the breakdown of my marriage, not taking away the blame from my husband who was too weak to stand up to them and be his own man.

There is also the umbilical cord which is never cut from Mummyji but instead becomes a noose around the daughter-in-law's neck. I've never understood why a husband needs to report the entire goings-on in his home and marriage to Mummyji? I understand attachment, but to such a degree that it destroys a marriage does not make any sense to me at all. Didn't anyone teach them that it is unhealthy? After all, how long can you take the comparison or smile through clenched teeth when everything is reported to your mother-in-law behind your back.

I personally think the best solution is that you should live in a separate house from your in-laws initially until your marriage settles down. If you can't stay separately, then you must ensure that your in-laws interfere as little as possible. Constant 'suggestions' usually only lead to what can be called marriage *interruptis*. After all, if an individual is old enough to get married, then they are old enough to be trusted to handle their own affairs, however messed up they may be. It's a sink or swim situation and a lot of marriages can swim if the in-laws allow them to.

In a divorce, your in-laws soon become outlaws in your life. Initially, my mother-in-law had taken my side and had reprimanded Paneer Boy for his behaviour. But when the petition was filed, I was shocked to learn that she had even produced my letters to her as evidence. These were loving letters I had written to her and she had shown them as proof of how good she was to me. It seemed like there was no dignity, honour or privacy during a divorce.

Nothing matters and even outlaws jump in the fray to grab the maximum brownie points of their offspring. Parents are willing to come to court and in fact, my mother-in-law did accompany her beloved son once. I felt pity for her because she looked frail and worried and I suddenly wished that they had not put her through this painful experience. Sometimes I think that parents suffer the most and experience even more pain than their progeny. They hold themselves responsible and think that they can change things and make them right for their children. It's like they regress to our childhood when they could make most of the things right for us.

In the court, the parents' role is lamentable as their creaky bones sit uncomfortably on crumbling chairs. They sometimes become menial workers for lawyers as they run around doing errands like photocopying. They hover around lawyers, literally begging them to save their child. They even chip in to pay the lawyer's fees. They are distraught and fraught with tensions and their health suffers sometimes

more than their children's. I know of two people who have
lost their parents to stress-related diseases—one had a stroke
and another a heart attack because they could not face the
reality of their children going through a divorce and the
pressures of dealing with the court. One of them even on
his deathbed in a delirious state kept on muttering about
his daughter's court date and how she must get free of the
torture of her case, talking to anyone who could help right
from relatives to people in court.

Finally, parents and family seek help from the Divine.
They consult astrologers and also perform poojas. One of
my aunts had offered to do a pooja on my behalf because
she had so much goodwill towards me. She was so persistent
that I went ahead and paid for the pooja. I don't think it
helped me because the divorce took so long that I went in
as a graduate and came out with a postgraduate degree *and*
still the case wasn't getting over.

So parents instead of relaxing in the evening of their lives
are trying to keep up with a changing world that they don't
understand. Instead of pampering their grandchildren, they
are fighting for custody and dealing with the added burden
of fixing up another marriage. One of the girls who came
to the support group told me that her father was selling his
posh flat in Worli and would move to a less posh locality
so that he could resettle the daughter. I wish the daughter
would work and look at maybe moving to another city. I
also wish that the parents would let her look after herself,
as they are in their seventies and they have already done
their bit for her. I wish they would let her carve out a new

life based on her preferences and capability and her own decisions—after all she was old enough to marry, have sex and have a kid—old enough to live her own life and pay for her own mistakes.

For my part, I was quite torn and feel betrayed that my in-laws who portrayed themselves as the upholders of honesty in their business dealings with the world, eventually did what the others do in this situation, back their child even if he was wrong. After all that I had known about them, they were supposed to be different, then how could they behave like the others. I thought they would at least insist honesty and would at least in private have a meeting with me and talk about the truth. After all, whatever is written in a petition isn't the entire truth. It is actually the contrary, especially with the embellishments by our overactive imagination and the lawyers' 'expertise'. They fell from my esteem when they acted just like the others. What hurts is that even before the petition was filed they didn't so much as bother to make a phone call to enquire about my well-being. All the lofty expositions before were then mere words. They appeared to be so concerned for my well-being initially, but I guess if you falter you become a persona non grata. They too prove that blood is thicker than water.

As for me, I only experienced one aspect of it as I am an orphan. For the first time in my life, I was thankful that my parents were not alive. I would have hated for them to experience even a greater anguish than me. Because the pain got exacerbated by the *khus phus,* idle gossip, outside the court and the socio-legal fall out of the system. Surely I would also not like to share with my parents what I was doing for sex all the while since this case was going on. That would not lead to khus phus but slap slap from them.

23

Let's Talk about Sex

It had been many years since my case had been going on with a separation of almost a year before that. I was a young woman at the peak of my youth. And sexual appetites differ in different stages of divorce. In the first phase you are ready to kill anyone who even remotely suggests sex, in the second phase you think about sex with your soon to be ex-spouse, in the third phase you wonder how you ever had sex with your soon to be ex-spouse, in the fourth phase you start thinking about sex as a possibility, in the fifth phase you really think of sex with someone else besides your soon to be ex-spouse and then finally you know that at least you are completely detached—at least physically—from your spouse and are ready to explore sexual possibilities with others. Now that my case had set into a monotonous pattern, I was ready to go on with my life. Is it not the natural thing for an emancipated woman of the nineties to want to lead an active sexual life? My sexual state was completely detached from the reality of my divorce. You don't expect hormones to understand that they aren't expected to be their own self. Life can be really ironic. In college, I was the one who would tell my boyfriend that I would wait and be 'the good girl' and I am sure that frustrated him to no end. But at that point, I felt it was the right thing to do.

And now, after a few years of my case languishing in the family court, I felt that going on a trip to London to meet up with an ex was the right thing to do. Literally and figuratively speaking. And so I met with an ex-boyfriend there, chatted, and of course did the deed and it felt so good. I felt so great and on top of the world and didn't feel so tight and wound up any more. It was a brilliant sensation and I felt benevolent towards the world at large. Just a body connecting with another . . . the touch, the sensation, the tingling of the skin, the tongues touching each there and exploring the mouths and then moving to other parts of the body and feeling each other's nooks and crannies so no part was untouched. The ecstasy and unadulterated joy of being naked and in each other's arms. It is like being transported to heaven. And lovemaking feels so devastatingly enjoyable. The touch of one on another, the friction and the melting of one's body into another and the amalgamation of the two bodies and just for that time, knowing what the other body wants and the undulation and the curves and grooves that meld and weld into one another. All your senses are electrifyingly alive.

Is it love or lust? This was when I reflected years later because at that time there was no need to. Did I feel guilty? Did I feel that I had done something wrong? Was I a fallen woman? Did I do the moral thing and after this would my moral compass go haywire? I know I am a modern, independent woman in charge of my life but that did not mean that I would be jumping into bed with any and everybody. I am human and however impenetrable my body suit of bravery is, certain questions of morality and what is right or wrong do pop up in my mind. So many questions and what were the answers. I only know one—I needed the intimacy.

After all, you do get lonely and that can be devastating. It's like you are in a roomful of people and you are alone and yet you know you are not. How much can only platonic friendship fill the deep grooves in your bed and body and the cracks in your heart? How do you deal with the lingering feeling of emptiness which sometimes can only be alleviated by a warm body? So, after my initial moral dilemma I felt nothing of the so called guilt.

After London, I realized that there was something wrong with a legal system which had cases going on forever and still gave no respite to the parties to carry on with their lives and at least engage in sex with a partner of their choice without fear of having it held against you in court. Why should my sexual appetite be repressed because I am going through a divorce? Will someone please stand up and change this godforsaken, archaic system. You tell me is it fair that we come into the courts as young people and leave as people who have had the joy of life sucked out of them? Should we reject intimacy because the system forbids it or because we fear that we may lose the case and maybe be in the judge's bad books? Even the lawyers caution you about conducting liaisons. I'd like to see them be single for a long time. But life had to continue and it did.

My new lawyer only asked me to be cautious about any relationships and liaisons but never discouraged me against them. So all in all I was set for the next level for my case and in some ways my life. My support group was going well and was not only helping people but also helping me both emotionally and publicly because it was featured in the press. This helped me quell all the so-called character blotches that the divorce petition alleged I had. Even my job was going well, so I didn't have much to complain about except the fact that I seemed to be in a state of limbo and had to spend a lot of time in attending the court and also thinking about freedom. I just wanted this to end so that I could get on with my life. It's not hampering your day-to-day existence but is for sure a mental block to continue leading a so-called normal life. Of course, it did impede your travel because you had to ensure you were in court for the dates, and yes, for things like not spending too much money so as to not appear to be a fool in court whilst asking for alimony. It also meant that your social life was to be constantly watched and of course unbelievable sex was always to be done with caution, or sneakiness. I just didn't like the sneaking part at all. I am an honest person and didn't see the need for two consenting adults to go about like skunks to do it.

The system should probably have a time frame of perhaps a year after a case has started and then allow litigants to lead their own lives and if that involves having sex then you can do so without any repercussions. If you don't want to, that also is your choice, but it should not be a moral regulation imposed on us by the court. We must work towards changing this system which forces us to lie and be slaves to this so-called code of morality that no one in their right mind should endorse.

I am only expressing what others want to do, but don't say it. It's sad but true that they keep mum because they are scared of being branded a whore or a woman of loose morals. I am sure so many of us do want to break free from these sanctimonious codes imposed on us.

Was this divine sex for real? Dreams are not confined by the shackles of reality. You know imagination and biological needs cannot be chained by the laws of the land, or society, or the lawyers. Till the system changes, I dream of my fast and furious, unencumbered ecstatic SEX . . . court case or not, while the rest of my life would keep going on from date to date, work, social life, home, friends, relatives, bad times and good.

24

Sweet and Sour—Life Goes On

I heard something amazing the other day, 'The graveyard is full of indispensable people' which makes you realize that life does go on, whether we like it or not. Time does not stop but you may be lost and buried under the hands of time unless you are willing to take the bull by its horns and move on.

My divorce proceedings were continuing and so was my life; life doesn't stop and if we don't accept that, we are the foolish ones who will suffer. I didn't have a routine of sorts but on a day-to-day basis would go for work, come back in the evening and have tea and snacks and go off to the club. In fact, Khar Gymkhana, despite all its various other aspects, has for me proved a home that provided me shelter in my toughest of times. Even though Paneer Boy had given a letter stating that I should not be allowed to use the club facilities, the club president at that time took a very progressive stand and said, 'She is not yet divorced, and since the matter is subjudice, let her use the club.' I said that I would pay my own club bills and he was quite impressed by this.

So being progressive does not mean wearing short skirts or having a six pack or doing coke. It means being forward thinking for the right kind of reasons such as siding with a girl in this predicament. Like my mum used to say, 'Just because I don't wear a mini does not mean that I am not modern and will stop my daughter from studying ahead or having a boyfriend.' Progressive is being so in thoughts and actions, not merely appearances. This in fact turned the tide in my favour in the court, since the club was a major player in the petition and my behaviour in it was used to portray me as a club and bed hopper. This made the judge realize that if my behaviour was so appalling the club itself would have suspended me on some pretext and not taken this discretionary action in my favour.

I also used to go out a lot with my friends and made quite a few 'going out' friends. These were my friends in coffee shops, a couple of clubs, some libraries, work and also nightclubs. It felt nice to be free and not talk about my ongoing state of affairs. I would, even when going out with them, ensure that I paid my own bills and when we went to a five-star hotel, I would beg off eating as I didn't want to spend so much and didn't want to impose on my friends' kindness. One just learns to adjust. Life is a great teacher if you are willing to learn.

The thing about divorce is that you must not become obsessed with punishing the other party. You are no one to decide on meting out any form of justice and to take on the role of a vigilante. Maybe it is also your fault. After all, you just can't clap with only one hand. It should not become an overriding concern to teach the other person a lesson. In fact, you must have a life outside the court. The court is a small part of your life, though painful, but it should not be the only life you know. I once asked one of my support group friends about what she did after her court date was over. She said, 'Go back home and mark the next date in the calendar and wait for that one, to meet my husband and torture him by not allowing him to meet the children.' I was horrified that the only life she looked forward to was the life she didn't have. This is such a sad waste of life and she should have moved on. By this, I don't mean taking it lightly but to let go of things. You are only harming yourself by letting a wound fester instead of treating it. It has become a diseased part of your life and at some level you should amputate it. This is the best way to preserve yourself and your dignity, and maybe, somewhere down the road also rise above this pettiness. You should ask yourself if you want someone to be the centre of your life when you are not even a part of their life any more. Playing the blame game is foolish and the only ones who benefit are the lawyers. What does it matter, who broke whose heart, mind, body and soul? The fact is now it is broken and even if it was mended it would have cracks in it. So go ahead, get a new heart, a new life, with or without anyone else, you deserve it. This should not be the be all and end all of your life. Let your bad relationship with your spouse not define you and you shouldn't turn into the Wicked Witch of the West and persecute him endlessly. Relationships do not end just because there is a divorce. A judge once remarked that just because you are divorced doesn't mean that all other relationships do not exist. You will still be the aunt for the kids in your ex-husband's family.

An important consideration in a divorce is children. The child not only suffers from a broken psyche but is sometimes unable to speak or even express his true feelings. I am not an expert to talk on children since I didn't have any of my own but from what I have seen, they are torn apart when asked to choose between parents and take sides. Many a times, they are forced to take sides and sit in judgement. They are too young to be a part of this, mere pawns to satisfy the parents. Let them have a normal childhood and let them not pay for their parents' mistakes. A classic example was when one of my support group friends called and said, 'I am very worried that my son is refusing to get married. He is totally against it.' I laughed sardonically and said, 'Did you expect anything else when you feed him on a diet of venom against the father and your miserable marriage.' Children should be fed love and affection not arsenic and cyanide even if their parents are two separate entities.

So all the normal things in life began again and I was quite happy that despite being alone I did not begin each conversation with the injustices of Prem Cheapda and

Paneer Boy and had not become a cynic. No one is at fault and you just have to accept this as a gash in your life.

The biggest change that happened in my life was absolutely positive. I am pretty sure that if my marriage would not have reached an end, I wouldn't have ever put pen to paper and taken up writing, at first to vent out and later as a profession. I come from a family where no one is a writer. In fact, in my mum's family the joke is that most of them haven't even read a complete book and here I go and write one. They are more interested in reading the account books—there favourite book being the cheque book—than literary books. After all, in their world there are only five letters—M–O–N–E–Y.

I started writing initially because I really had no one to confide in, so the 'Dear Diary' became an important part of my life. Then I had to document the experiences of the support group members so it became imperative to write. When doing so, I realized that most of those in our position have similar stories, questions and situations and that this information needed to be shared. So I became a writer by default. Though I must admit that my dad was an avid reader and he would have been so proud of me today. I bet he would have said proudly that his daughter is an author. There is a bright side to every incident in life and it is your job to find it and make it work for you. No point in crying and sobbing and cursing. Instead you should turn the negative into positive and make it count. After all, success is the best revenge.

I studied law and completed the course. So now I am

a qualified lawyer and also an honest one. My work with the United Nations, another job I got after my marriage broke up, also featured me in the press. I would be lying if I don't confess that I got a big kick out of it, especially the first time. The articles appeared with regularity and I didn't even have a PR agent—actually didn't have money for one. Then my articles appeared for Lead India and then the book and the support group because no one wanted to talk about the divorce. I am telling you all this not to show off (okay, I am showing off a little, wouldn't you if you were in my place) but to let you know that so many achievements can also happen along the way if your self-belief is consistent. So again, all this was happening because I allowed myself to move on in life.

I also feel that all my experiences helped shape my individuality and I became an entity of sorts in my own eyes. I grew beyond just looks to someone with substance. I felt that I had earned my right to call myself my parents' daughter. I believe I wouldn't have done so many things if my marriage was good. So one just thinks that there is a positive flip on most things in life, you only have to catch that. I have been careful to continue living and not just be a tombstone with court dates engraved on me.

★★★

In this Kafkaesque, emotionally wringing, turbulent phase of my life I am sure I would have been unable to make it through without the presence in my life of His Holiness the Dalai Lama, Sadhviji, Sadhuji, Babaji, His Eminence

Tsugla Lopen Samten Dorji . . . the names are so many and
the forms so many but they all lead to the same one, the
one and only God. Everything begins and ends with Her.
So She has been with me and all of us through thick and
thin and in so many ways and forms that it is difficult to
comprehend what we would do without Her. I feel God is
a woman (after all she is unpredictable and if you piss her
off you are dead, just like with a woman), but that is the
debate for another time.

It is quite amazing that you can ultimately count on God
for your share of unconditional support, love, direction, to
talk your heart out, for guidance, for the unfairness of it
all, for sharing your grief and for happiness. How many
times have I beat my chest very dramatically and told Her
that she was being unjust and cruel and had become deaf
and blind to my sorrows and was siding with the villains.
I have even mourned the changing world where it pays
to lie and you are penalized for being honest and sticking
to your principles—look at Aung Sang Suu Kyi, Nelson
Mandela. I have lamented the greediness and callousness
of the rich where they make their own rules and are never
punished and get away with murder or something akin to
what my in-laws were doing in my case. When I failed to
get answers, I begged Her to at least stop it.

You pray to a God based on faith and you can't see
anyone or hear anything and only look for signs that your
prayers have been answered and live on faith. I prayed to
Her on the day my interim maintenance was to be heard
and I heaved a sigh of relief when I saw the evidence of

Her presence. I had been granted a princely sum and that too in retrospect. There is a God and there is justice. I prayed when I was evicted from Khar Gymkhana for no fault of mine except that the committee president knew my father-in-law and I was told to leave the club and that too with the public notices. I prayed for strength.

And no, I didn't pray with lofty ideals like asking for forgiveness for my enemies but for the whole of the Prem Cheapda gang to vanish like a nightmare. I am no Mother Teresa to forgive the whole world and their grandfather. But I was sure that I would not pursue a negative path to teach them a lesson or plot their downfall. In life you have to chalk out your path based on positive thoughts and actions.

I also thanked Her when my prayers were answered and also when I hadn't prayed for great things and they happened anyways like a job in America or meeting a nice guy who would make me laugh and not paw me and expect something more from an evening just because we had had a good time and maybe because he had paid for my dinner. I feel Her presence throughout even if I didn't want it and maybe it was because of meditation or because I had no one. My dependence was strong and I never debated whether a God existed or not though I did question Her ways.

I feel meditation helps and it calms you and helps to focus inside and look at your life for other meanings than revenge and hatred. Over time, this enabled me to get over the blind hatred of my hubby and in-laws and helped me to even forgive them and laugh at their idiosyncrasies like photocopying over and over again every demand draft they gave me and making me sign them. I was able to get past their absolute refusal to look at only their view as right, their stodgy beliefs that women should only wear Indian clothes and working in a school would be the only independent working life they would allow.

My hatred was replaced by humour thanks to the Almighty. Over a period of time God has helped me to find jobs, get by in life, make and keep friends, and avoid relatives. She has also helped me to make my peace and move on by opening other doors and windows for me. She has helped me not only survive but also live well and be a winner even in my own eyes and perhaps in the world's as well. I have healed the scars and wounds and sometimes even forgotten about them and truly moved on and made lemonade from lemons. I have never forgotten the mere presence of the being which helped me to achieve this state. I am grateful for this and I am able to be in this enlightened state where not only have I made peace with my situation but hopefully helped others along the way. Some have held my hand and some have left it and I think I may have left the hands of some others but my life has been an onwards journey and not backwards. I have only looked at the past for learning and not with regret except, of course, a couple of things, but then to be human is to have regrets.

God has been my armour and protective sheath and my unflinching belief in the Almighty has led me to a higher path and helped me in my journey of self-realization. I have won some and lost some, learnt some and forgotten some but all-in-all I have survived this cycle of life living well and by being well-loved. Though I am hopeful that the 360 degrees of divorce for me would end now that a decade has gone by and as my eyes scan the wall calendar I realize that D Day is here.

25

Virgin Once Again

The entire decade of my divorcologue sped through my mind with clarity as I sat in the divorce court. I blanked out everything except the travels and travails of my divorce. Over a decade ago was my D-day—marriage—and now this was another D-day—divorce. The past ten years of the entire divorce saga just melted and dissolved into a reality that had brought me here today. They say that your entire life flashes before you just before you die and the same was happening to me as my marriage was officially dying and I was being given a new life, except that after this death I was still alive and hadn't gone to heaven or hell. But I had faced my own hell and created a heaven out of it. I had come in as a defeated woman but was leaving with my head held high in pride, my dignity and dreams intact. My dreams were waiting to create a new reality for me where

I was to be the Mistress of my own destiny. As I set about carving a new life for myself, I heard the booming voice of the judge.

'*I now pronounce you non-man and non-wife,*' is what I thought I heard.

Shouldn't divorce decrees read like that, now the wedding knot was untied? With this you could soon undo the entire past and restart life all over again, without even any memory of what happened. Alas! That is not how real life works.

We were waiting on the 4th floor of the court to go to the counsellor to complete the formality of divorce now that we had converted the petition into a divorce by consent. Then I smiled as I saw the buck-toothed peon who had been transferred to this floor. He was giving me a toothy grin and guiding me into the counsellor's office. He knew I had been coming for years and had seen my frustrations and must've been sympathetic to my plight. So much time had passed that the staff had gone through two to three transfers for the entire duration that my case had been going on. The sad part is that the case had not even reached the 'argument stage in court' (legally speaking) in ten years as both of us had taken advantage of every loophole in law to delay it or was it the other way round? Maybe we thought we were in a win–win situation?

As we were ushered into the counsellor's office we were asked to be seated. The counsellor smiled at me, the smile of acknowledgement that you give a regular. Yes, if you go to a place for a decade you do become a regular. I couldn't believe it that I had been coming to the family court in Bandra for a decade.

The counsellor's office had not changed in a decade, after all it is a government office. She then proceeded with the formalities. She asked me, 'Are you consenting to give a divorce?' I answered in the affirmative. She then asked Paneer Boy the same question and he said like an eager beaver, 'Yes.' I couldn't hide my smile at his excitement. Then the lawyers from both sides took out the consent petition which had been prepared before and was barely a two-pager. This was no comparison to the actual divorce petition, which ran into fifteen foolscap pages and along with the other petitions and counter petitions filed, I could have easily netted about Rs 1000 from the junk seller.

So this piece of paper would've changed my life because I would now no longer be *Mrs*, just a *Miss*. All the other petitions had kept my status as a suspense. This chit of a paper did change it. After all, good things do come in small packets.

Then of course I couldn't resist telling Paneer Boy, 'I think you should tell Daddy (on purpose I called my father-in-law as such because I knew it would irritate him) that six months have passed long time ago, and I was waiting for him to have got you the divorce on the dot of six months. Tell him it just got delayed by nine and a half years.' PB was seething with anger and I was almost certain that he may change his mind. He just grunted.

Then came the handing over of the alimony amount which was made as a demand draft, which didn't even cover a fraction of what I had spent on the marriage, and he had got six copies of it. I wished that he had given me six cheques instead, so I would get six times the amount—*that* would have been nice. He made me sign an acknowledgement on every copy and peered closely at every signature as though I meant to sign in invisible ink. When he noticed that my signature was slightly different on one, he started shouting and tried to grab the original from my hand. The counsellor was horrified and said, 'We are there so don't worry about anything and keep your voice down.' I just said, 'Calm down, I will sign it again,' and I did. But that one act of his convinced me that I'd done the right thing.

That one act of his defined his personality and our marriage. He was aggressive and this marriage was always based on suspicion.

That one act of his cracked the façade that he wore of a gentleman stuck with the wrong woman who he tried to portray as a gold-digger.

That one act of his showed his obsession with money.

That one act of his reiterated to me that he was still like a clockwork mouse wound by his father and would never ever change.

That one act of his showed me that if for such a petty amount he could react like this he would never take risks in life and would always be a mediocre, safe player.

That one act of his illustrated to me and all those present that what they were saying in the petition was baseless, what I was saying in the petition wasn't baseless.

That one act was an affirmation of his hatred for me and how impossible he found even parting with a farthing for me.

That one act of his displayed the violence that he was capable of. If he could behave like this in public, what would he be like in private; only I had seen and experienced that nightmare.

That one act was a confirmation for me that I did the right thing by being divorced from this man.

My lawyer tried to defuse the situation by saying, 'Okay, now kiss each other goodbye,' which at least made everyone laugh. We stepped out of the chamber and I was smiling. I called the peon and tipped him and he smiled and asked me if everything had gone well. I said yes and then also called the other peons who had been helpful to me and tipped them. Then I went to the canteen on the first floor and for the last time in this court. I ate a dosa and drank lassi. This had become another home for me and I had in a strange way got attached to it. I even went and used the smelly loo. Eventually my lawyer said, 'Vandana, you need to go home now.' I looked at her and hugged her and I had tears in my eyes because if she hadn't been there, this entire experience would've been even more disastrous for me, considering the illegal expertise of my first lawyer.

I stepped out but just before doing so did the unthinkable. Yes a hygiene freak like me actually kissed the paan-stained, dirty, filthy wall of the family court as a final adieu. But you know, a large part of my adult life was spent in this place. Boy! It had become like a tooth cavity, where you keep putting your tongue in the cavity because it feels weird and hurts a bit but you are addicted to it. Something like a dog licking its wound, it's painful but he can't stop doing it. Then I headed to the car park and tipped the car guy and told him my case was over and he said, 'You must have won. I prayed for you every time.' I was overwhelmed by his concern and could really feel the tears welling up in my eyes as I thought this can only happen in the diverse and varied and beautiful country— India—a mixed bag of contradictions, at once kind and the next instant cruel, indifferent yet caring, slow yet fast, God fearing yet dishonest, but the social fibre of bonds between people never wavering. I went to the temple where I used to go each time before I entered the court and said a 'Thank you'. Then came back again to the car and drove off home. It was over and I must admit that though I thought I would experience an emptiness since this was such a part of my life, yet I felt nothing but ecstasy as I drove really fast and reached home and just hit my bed.

That night I lay in bed thinking that the time that had elapsed did show on my face in some laughter lines and some excess weight, but those are just physical evidences which can be undone. The mental and emotional changes are vast. I was a bit wiser, a bit maturer but definitely not a cynic as I still looked at life through rosy spectacles. I had vowed even at the beginning that I would not be a pessimist but would continue to look at the glass as half full. I continue to do so. I had learnt so much along the way, life's experiences, how to conduct myself fearlessly through life. I knew now that nothing in life could defeat me. I also had a newfound respect for myself as I had stood up for myself and proved even the worst of my critics wrong.

I had definitely fought on the principle of not wanting to give in just because my head was being ground in the grindstone and I didn't. I had fought with all my might and had won when I was the dark horse and had minimal resources. Yes, my self-respect and dignity were sky high. I still remember the day my father-in-law had flicked me off as a fly saying, 'We will get the divorce in six months and you won't even know!' Well, surely that hadn't happened. I had stood my ground and won. Won in a different sense as in a divorce case no one wins .After all two lives are going through the wringer. But my principles of not cowering in fear when faced with a challenge, had stood the test of time. I had really proved to myself that even though I hadn't fought a war like my dad but I was an Air Force officer's daughter—fearless and brave and willing to fight the odds in life.

I would be free to now live a life I choose and I have. The horizons for me are endless and I feel God has given me an opportunity to restart again at the end of a rainbow clutching my pot of gold (though I can assure you that the alimony would not even be able to buy a gold-plated pot). I was now FREE . . . FREE . . . FREE . . .

26

Eno-cent Divorcee

Men, money, peace, weight loss, peace, dancing, roaming, more friends, no looking over the shoulder to see if you are being followed by anyone—actual FREEDOM. So what does life after the divorce taste like?

The best way to describe it would be to liken it to a triple ice-cream sundae on a hot day. I could go out any time I liked, befriend anyone and generally have a good time. I could even be looking at working overseas, which I did for some time, without the fear of a new court date looming overhead. I was actually free and not dependent on a government employee for deciding my fate now. No more crosses and checks on my calendar and the best part, no more shitty rags to wear. I said goodbye to the widowed look and embraced a new me.

I could now even reciprocate the flirtation of the men

without any guilt. I went out on romantic dates to fun places. And, it sure was romantic. I dressed up and looked gorgeous and felt even more so. I had a few flings which were satisfying and did wild things in bed that I didn't even know I was capable of, and all because of my hubby, at least, indirectly. Life was definitely looking up.

I had fun with my relatives too. They were desperate to know the alimony amount and I told them so many different figures that I am sure they were more confused after my disclosure than before it. They pretended to be happy but obviously weren't and their questions about the alimony took so many forms that it was fun to watch them.

I remember a conversation when my aunt was pestering me for the alimony amount. I suddenly asked her, 'Why do you all hate me so much?' At first she tried to lie and this charade continued for an hour. Then when I refused to accept anything but the truth I think something cracked inside her and she spoke, 'You always had it easy in life. Your mom pampered you and you always got what you wanted. You did well in college, always had the best clothes and looked so good effortlessly and fought a lot for your mother and also loved her a lot. You had the ideal life and were so arrogant that we have always tried to bring you down because you had it all. No one got it as good as you.'

I was shocked and had tears in my eyes. 'All in life. You think I had it all in life. I worked damn hard at studying and managed to look good in minimal expense. I had to look after Mummy in hospital when she was dying of cancer and lost my Dad also to cancer at the age of sixteen and you are telling me I had it good. I paid the heaviest price in life as I lost both my parents at such a young age and literally had no youth as I had to skip immediately into responsibility. Try giving up a career in modelling and any other career when you are not even nineteen as the choices you have are between looking after your mum, whose body is wracked by the poisonous cells and she is in constant pain, and between working out of the house. She was leaving me and I had to smile because I couldn't show her my pain and had to smile to keep her in good spirits as the doctor had given up hope long time ago and the only thing he had told me to do was to keep her happy and you are telling me I had it really easy. What a joke. Sure, I was brave, but that is how I have always been. I just didn't speak up because in life you have to fight your own battles, so you don't tell me that I had a real cushy life.' I couldn't believe that I was sobbing as I said this.

She just looked at me agape.

I went into the other room and she asked me no other questions and just bid me goodbye and left, all 200 tonnes of her body left my house. I just felt relieved and this outburst also made me feel lighter. I don't think it would change my relatives and really nothing would. I feel maybe some learning from their children's lives will bring changes in theirs.

I ran my support group diligently, and considered many times of making it a paid-for service. But every time I heard the sadness and helplessness in the voices of those desperate girls I would decide not to. I went ahead and attended all the lectures and sessions for helping those who needed it and they turned up in large numbers which further reiterated my belief that people do require such a service for sure. I went through so much that along with the case I did my law degree and am now a full-fledged lawyer. What sort of a lawyer am I? I will let my clients decide, but money is not my motivator and I treat all my cases as human beings and not case numbers. My new firm for which I have done only free cases so far is called . . . you guessed it right . . . 360 Degrees Back to Life.

I became a little bit maturer and have learnt to take disappointments in my stride. I realized I was no longer that girl who was the topper throughout and now had this thing which wasn't perfection—*Chand me daag* (even the moon has blemishes). I looked at people like my sister who said they will not sponsor me to Australia because her husband basically hates me but she said that he wanted me to get married and then he'd do it and because he felt that I would come between his wife and him and all such other reasons and maybe I would cause a divorce like divorce is a contagious disease that if you get you can pass it to on others. I pity them and am not angry with them, as I would have been ten years ago before the case had started.

I also went out a lot with my friends and really reconnected with them. I discovered why we had become friends and why the friendship had endured. We rediscovered the simple joys of what we had in school and college. I listened to a lot of music with or without them and created music for my life. The best thing was that I discovered that I could write and I wrote all the time, no holds barred. Writing became my single pleasure and was sometimes so exciting that I almost thought feeling this way was illegal. I wrote a few manuals, wrote a book, edited others' works and found my calling in life.

I also started working on an environment technology endorsed by the United Nations, which was again an achievement in itself. From thereon it was a slow and steady rise to the top, work-wise. I started writing and really discovered my true passion for it—like they say, if your passion is your profession, you are never working. The crowning glory for my work was when BBC approached me to film a documentary about my work for women going through divorce and this was broadcast worldwide on International Women's Day and has been praised universally. The BBC documentary was really a turning point in my life and before I knew it I had turned a corner. The support group which started over a decade ago and has counselled over 5000 people till date in one-on-ones and in large groups was highly appreciated by all and especially by the BBC. They made a documentary about my work profiling me as a 'lone voice fighting an arduous battle bravely'. This had a viewership of millions.

The response was overwhelming and has made me an icon to others. But more than that, it has raised me in my own eyes, because after all, when you value yourself that is the greatest achievement.

The press coverage has been great and I don't even have a PR agent. Many journalists from various publications have written about my work and now a few of them are my friends. After all who doesn't like a story of grit and determination transcending adversity and coming out on tops—an underdog, who's not an underdog anymore.

I continue to run the support group, almost gratis, and the membership keeps growing. When people tell me that I changed their life, I am grateful that God has given an opportunity to change lives. But it's a cycle that continues, you help someone and someone helps you back and so on.

I also embarked on the journey of becoming a lawyer and am now practising in the family court. From what I hear, I have a clean and formidable reputation.

So my journey from litigant to lawyer has come a full circle in a decade.

I also participated in the Lead India and was selected as one eight finalists from Mumbai, which was a great high. During the course of this, I met Shobhaa Dé Ma'am who spotted a spark in me and has encouraged me to write and follow my destiny. Also Gloria Steinem has endorsed my book. What an exciting feeling it is when even others repose their faith in your abilities.

I also bring out a newsmagazine called *Ex-Files* which highlights the pitiable condition of divorce in India and spins some tales of bravery and a twang of humour in it, which has also met with success, so another feather in my cap!

What a walk it has been from a bank balance of Rs 750, alone and battered on that night a decade ago, to being feted by the BBC.

I also had some amount of lingering sadness in me—sadness for time wasted, for a life with a man which eventually had to be resolved in court. I also had a sense of loss in general, sadness for having to become what I did because of my experiences, for losing my youth, my new extended family, my precious time, a sense of innocence that I had gone through life, a distrust of relatives, dependence on strangers, the absence—actually complete absence—of the family, a sense of being a world in this world and facing everything on my own. But I continued to wear my rose-coloured spectacles and viewed life through those.

Spiritually and mentally I grew even without realizing it. My belief in the goodness of life remained unshakeable even in the darkest hours of the abuse. I know that good triumphs over evil, even if in the short term evil wins. The path of honesty may be laden with obstacles but one is a victor in the long run. I was also proud of myself that I stood for my principles in the case and won it without any deceit or resorting to falsehood or the usual tactics of filing for dowry or domestic violence.

My faith in following the right path got strengthened because I saw the rewards and am enjoying them today. My expectations from people dwindled but the faith in humanity and belief in God increased. I learnt to listen to the Universe because sometimes it has a deep message for you but we ignore and suppress it because we want to believe otherwise. I embraced failure with a feeling of equanimity knowing that success is round the corner. My faith in the karmic destiny, cycle of life was validated. My core strengthened with an unflinching belief in honesty, doing good, being fair, standing and fighting for your beliefs and, most of all, of just being a good human being. I did not lose my essence which is good, crazy, positive and depends on God for a bright, luminous, luminescent future.

Most of all I still live by my philosophy, 'I will rebuild my life by elevating myself rather than pulling down another.'

27

Uff—These Sections

Disclaimer: Even though I may have written the preceding chapters with a light pen to assuage the sting of the legal procedure, the legal process is a serious and well-developed process in India. Our able judiciary has given judgements that have even made the world sit up and take notice and laud the astuteness of the judges.

###★★★★!!!!>>>><<<<######^^^^^^^^^^^(((((
(((((★★★★★★★★######!!!!!!!????????????? This is how the legal sections seemed to me as I attempted to decipher their complicated meanings, their repercussions in court and what each one implied. All of them seemed so 'coma'plex, convoluted and life-threatening that if you made one wrong move you would lose your life. I had vowed to myself that if I ever wrote about them I would at least simplify these hieroglyphics so that if anyone is going

through a divorce they wouldn't die of fear or boredom or have a heart attack trying to decipher the sections.

With this aim in mind, I emailed a few lawyers and got my answers from Taubon Irani.

I went to interview her at the family court in Bandra, Mumbai, to get an understanding of the basic procedure of divorce. I was fed up of the legalese but still wanted to grasp what goes on in court.

I have simplified the legal terms, after all I am a divorce war veteran and where I had a doubt, I just piped in with questions to Taubon.

Process in court for divorce

1. Simply put, this just means you are going to litigate in court over the divorce because you still want to continue being married to your spouse for reasons best known to you.

    Filing of the petition is done by a petitioner who has to come in person and sign before the registrar in the family court.

    This is the primary step. In this the petitioner files for divorce after meeting his/her lawyer. The Advocate prepares his/her petition on instructions/information. This is the document that he/she will be filing in court as a first step to seek his/her divorce.

    This usually makes note of all the reasons for seeking a divorce. The contents are usually the incidents or reasons, actions and behaviour of both the parties which have lead to a disconnect and thereby the petitioner feels the need to seek the court's help for the termination of the marriage.

The incidents are supposed to reflect the truth, but in reality these are embellished to make the opposite party appear in an extremely bad light and to arouse the sympathy of the court for the petitioner. Although this is like a sworn affidavit yet the petitioner may tell a lie in it and usually the contents not only are exaggerated but are a lot of lies too.

The petition also illustrates the reasons for divorce be it adultery, insanity or desertion. These are usually the reasons which are the legal reasons as per the law of the land and the religion of the person or the 'Marriage Act' that they are married under.

This is signed and dated by the petitioner and identified by the lawyer.

This is then sent by registered post to the other party. At the time of filing, you give two copies of the petition along with the original one on Green Ledger paper. Once objections are removed from the petition, the petition is numbered and assigned a court. Before the first date, the petitioner or his lawyer collects the sealed packet from the court, which contains the petition along with the summons. The petitioner or his advocate then posts it by RPAD, sender's address being that of the court. The acknowledgement will be received directly by the court.

2. The first date is approximately after forty-five days due to rise in the number of petitions.

Since the rise in the number of petitions as well as to give sufficient time for service, the first date after receipt of the petition is after forty-five days. The increase in the number of divorces has led to the glut in the number of cases that come before the court. Currently the family court is the appropriate court to file the case in. Where there is no family court, it is filed in the district court of that area. Parsi matrimonial disputes are conducted in the High Court with a jury system.

The family court, in Mumbai, usually has about 50–60 cases, or matters as they are called, on board every day, on each floor and there are seven floors/courts with presiding judges so it is an average of about 200–250 cases a day. This is because sometimes a litigant will have two or three aspects of the case being mentioned on the same day so they get a different serial number; simply put, a litigant may be mentioned in two or more serial numbers on the same day. So even though there may be fifty matters in a day the cases are about thirty or forty. If a judge is absent then this creates a backlog and pushes up the number of cases even further. Hence the delay in cases.

This is a very practical problem and the courts must take positive action to resolve it. This becomes even more acute as it usually concerns personal matters and people's lives are on hold. Sometimes, you end up spending more time in a divorce case than being married—look at me!

3. Counsellors meeting on first date.

The litigants meet with the court-appointed marriage counsellor on the first date and thereafter, if there is a possibility of settlement, for two–three more dates till finalized. After a maximum of three dates the matter proceeds to court.

The counsellors listen to both sides. The first counselling is done singly and then together. This is done to give both of them a chance to express their point of view. Both are allowed to present their interpretation of facts and of course the facts. Usually the counsellors listen to them and then try their level best to see if the marriage can work or if the case is likely to be settled by consent or is going to be contested.

The counsellor files a report, after considering the matter, which is then sent to the judge. If the matter is not settled, then the counsellor merely states 'matter to proceed on merits'. If the matter is settled then consent terms are filed and you get a decree for divorce with the consent terms forming part of the decree.

4. Interim maintenance and interim custody filed on failure of counselling.

Court refers to parties to come to mutual agreement if possible or else decides on merit.

The applications for interim maintenance are filed, in which the wife asks for the monthly maintenance. This is usually granted to the wife when the case is going on and is calculated based on the earnings of the husband.

The interim custody remains with the custodial parent. Interim access is given to non-custodial parent. Custody at the end usually remains with the mother, more so if it is a daughter. Even before the arguments start in the main matter the court tries to get the parties to agree or then listens to both sides and decides the matter on its merits.

5. The meetings with the children are in the children's complex.

    If the wife alleges that the husband has a history of violence or if a father has not met his child for long, there is a children's complex which is on the third floor of the court building.

    Ideally both parents have equal access, i.e. weekends, 50 per cent of vacations. But certain mothers use the children as scapegoats to extort money from husbands and they cause hurdles in access.

6. Once interim applications are decided, issues are framed and the matter proceeds for evidence of petitioner.

    Framing of issues can be understood as the 'issues in the petition'.

    When the issues are framed the case is taken forward by the petitioner's lawyer in court who then leads the evidence of the petitioner. The examination-in-chief has to be in tandem with the petition filed. After issues, on the next date the petitioner files an affidavit in lieu of examination-in-chief along with a list of documents and list of witnesses, if any. Even the respondent files documents.

7. Cross-examination.

This is the part you see in Hindi movies where the hero usually questions the criminal with a lot of gestures and hand movements. The criminal lies but the hero nabs him with his expert questions.

Minus the dramatics, in fact, cross-questioning is the most difficult and also interesting aspect of a case and usually it does help to uncover the truth and the kernel of the case. This is all the more so when the lawyer is an expert.

The witnesses of the petitioner are produced after cross-examination of the petitioner is closed. These are questioned both by the petitioner's lawyer and the respondent's lawyer.

8. Thereafter evidence of the respondent and the same procedure as above.

When the issues are framed these are produced by the respondent's lawyer in court who then leads the evidence of the respondent. The examination-in-chief has to be in tandem with the written statement. Then witnesses of the respondent are produced after cross-examination of the respondent is over.

9. After both the parties' evidence is over, the matter is

placed for final arguments. Then the judge decides the matter on the basis of evidence and its merits.

10. Custody of the child/children generally remains with the mother unless due to extreme circumstances. (Like if the mom is a destitute, adulterous, has vices, is of unsound mind or a drug addict, etc.) Maintenance and alimony vary according to the facts of each case.

I have avoided going into all the minute details. I write as a litigant who wants to know what are the main things she needs to know in a divorce case. In fact I have presented an eagle's eye view of the procedure and have avoided going into the technicalities.

So next time your lawyer does *dadagiri* (bullying) in court do some 'legal name dropping' from my chapter.

28

Let's Play Dodge Ball with the Hydra-headed Monster

I had the feeling all throughout the court case that we are like caged animals in the divorce court. Would we ever get out, I wondered? If we did how will we get out unscathed and unhurt? But then going through the process myself I realized that the bars in the cage are not made of iron but of plasticine and can be stretched and moulded to any shape thanks to the judicial system.

Ladies and gentlemen, presenting before you, the Loopholes in Law!!!

Classification 1
Those used by men

How do the husbands avoid giving money?

Ever tried squeezing blood out of stone? That is easier than getting a husband to pay any kind of money, be it for interim maintenance, child support or alimony. I have discussed in detail how my husband tried to avoid paying me an interim maintenance. He not only exaggerated my tangible financial assets in court, putting a very heavy price tag on them which was far from their actual worth but also listed my intangible assets as a category. These included my soft skills which would help me get hired for a job, my education and also my talents for creating wealth. As I mentioned, these of course only came into play when it was time for him to shell out money, before that I was a complete no-gooder, worthless and incapable of doing anything right. This was also mentioned in the petition as an excuse to get a divorce and of course was *not* brought forth while arguing in court for the interim maintenance.

This is an oft used technique employed by husbands to get away without paying.

In fact, one wealthy business family of jewellers ended up paying less than Rs 700 per month to the wife.

They conjure up parents who are dependent on them, never mind that they don't bother about them otherwise. Once they are able to show dependents, they can avoid paying the wife as the disposable income is lesser.

They also transfer all their assets to other people's names. This includes their house, their car, money in the bank account. They even go to the extent of producing on paper that they are not the owners of their company but are mere employees to avoid paying money. Once they show themselves as employees, it is easier to take a pay cut and show that they are earning lesser than they actually are. I have even known men to have quit their jobs to avoid paying their wives. It is sad that they will trust anyone else with their money but they don't want to pay their wives. One interesting case came to me and during the course of the case the husband who had transferred his house to his brother's name really got his karma to come back to bite him in the bum, when his brother absolutely refused to acknowledge that the house was transferred to his name to just tide over the 'minor' problem of paying the wife. Oh, how we laughed till our sides ached. Now her husband was homeless and could do nothing to get it back. He had transferred his house willingly and had ensured that all the paperwork was legal. So there was no way he could claim that he did it under duress. Wow! What interesting ways things work out sometimes. Even if we had scripted this we couldn't have asked for a better ending.

Why do I say better ending? Because his wife was so desperate that she was living in a rented apartment and working as a housekeeper in a hotel because she wasn't qualified enough to be back in the job market. She had been married for a decade and used to work as an airhostess. She had to settle for this job as she had a child to feed. Shouldn't he have been fair to his wife and at least provided her with a roof over her head? I do know that she managed to get a decent alimony and did her MBA by correspondence. So now she is working in a call centre and is earning a fair amount of money.

I have shared this incident to illustrate the extent the husband will go through to avoid paying the wife—so the wife needs to be smart.

Solution and Safety Measures: When things aren't well in the marriage, make an effort to upgrade your skills. At this stage, maybe you should even try and have access to your husband's money. Be aware of his finances. Don't be foolish and completely clueless.

In case you have a joint account in a marriage that is going sour, or if the divorce petition has been filed, don't hesitate to withdraw the money from the account and keep it aside for a rainy day. Believe me, the expenses of a lawyer and also keeping home and your daily life can be crippling; this money will come in handy. This may sound harsh yet it will be a lot better than what you will have to face later if you are left penniless. This is a pragmatic way of looking at things and one has to be so when your life is involved.

A number of times, women take the moral higher ground—I can earn my own money and I don't need his. But don't think that you don't deserve his money—even a servant is paid and you have been his wife. And no matter how bad a wife you may have been at least you must have performed some wifely duties, so accept this money as a payment. If your conscience still pricks you, well then be an angel and return the money when you are flush with funds. (In my ten years of counselling, I have never ever come across such a case. The day that happens fairy tales will come true and I will be Sleeping Beauty, sleeping through my marriage and the divorce proceedings.)

Oh yes! Only in films poverty and unnecessary struggle seem glamorous and even that has changed now to reflect the times that we live in.

HUF: The HUF is the Hindu United Family which, putting it simplistically, could own the family assets. The woman cannot ask for division in the assets and ask to be separated with her share. Earlier even this was a way of avoiding paying the wife, since the majority of the assets were held in the HUF and the husband claimed that he could not ask for a division due to the legalities involved. I have only put forth the basic facts about HUF as it has many facets, one of which is that it is employed as an instrument to avoiding paying the wife.

Now things have changed a bit as the combined worth of the HUF is taken into consideration by the judge when ordering the payment of alimony.

In my case, we had valiantly fought for the HUF to be taken into consideration but since we settled it without going into a later stage, we didn't refer to it further.

Solution and Safety Measures: When there is trouble in the marriage, please be aware that the HUF exists and about an approximate amount of money and properties tied up in it. This is somewhat similar to the previous solution emphasizing on awareness as opposed to complete ignorance.

Classification 2
Loopholes used by women

Even women misuse the law, so it's not that we are all sugar and spice and everything nice.

Misuse of the Domestic Violence Act: Even women misuse certain aspects of the law. One of them is the Domestic Violence Act, which in its basic form provides protection to women from violence. Victims can seek protection in law and usually the recourse to law also grants them the right to stay in the matrimonial home. This may also get the husband and in-laws to be removed from the matrimonial home. However, now the law only grants her the right to do so if the home is in her husband's name.

This is for the simple reason that women were taking undue advantage of the law and even literally throwing out their in-laws on the roads. One couple in their late seventies was thrown out by their daughter-in-law under the pretext of the DV Act and they were shattered because it was a ruse to get them out and their son was involved. The couple was shattered not only by their actual eviction but also by their son's betrayal.

The cases where this Act has been misused have been many and it defeats the purpose of the Act. But I would still say that this is better than not having any recourse to law. Plus the percentage of women misusing it is very minuscule in comparison to the women who are actually suffering. I guess bad apples are there everywhere. I am not justifying the misuse but it is better to take the chance to protect the oppressed and if some cunning people take advantage one has to discount them as exceptions to the rule.

Solution and Safety Measures: A word of caution for the parents. Please do not transfer your property on your child's name while you are alive, they will have plenty of time later once you are not there. Why not be safe so that you are not on the streets because of the connivance of your son and daughter-in-law.

I'm afraid I can offer no solution to the husbands in this instance.

Dowry: Usually in court cases a number of women end up reporting that the husband and the in-laws are demanding dowry and lodge a complaint in the police station. Once that happens, the accused have to spend a night in the care of the government in the police station. One of my acquaintances from the support group and his sixty-five-year-old mother were arrested on a Friday night and they got no bail on Saturday and hence spent three nights in jail. In fact, getting an arrest warrant on Fridays is an old trick used by the lawyers so that instead of one day, three days are spent in jail.

Although this is misused, one must keep in mind the genuine cases and also of course the high number of dowry deaths and suicides by married girls who don't want to burden their parents for dowry. So again, one has to keep these provisions in law for protection of women.

Solution and Safety Measures: There are certain changes in law so men need to be aware of these.

Better still, if your marriage is turning sour and if your wife is willing to give you an affidavit that you have not taken any dowry, you can take that.

Other than these there are not many measures I can offer.

Custody of children: This is also a tool used by women not only to extort money when the case is going on but also once they are divorced. I have absolutely nothing but repulsion for women who practise such undignified stunts. They end up destroying their children's lives and instead of nurturing them with love, feed them with acid and arsenic. Let the children decide on their own what they want and what each parent stands for.

I know of a case—let's call her Komal (which means soft, but she is the opposite). She has tutored her daughter, who is about seven years old, to touch the judge's feet when she comes to court and then wail loudly when she sees her father in court and beg not to have to see him. Sad, after all, if he hadn't made his contribution towards having the child, Komal wouldn't be a mother. He should be allowed to be a father as well.

Solution and Safety Measures: There is none except telling the child the truth and hoping as he or she grows older that they differentiate fact from fiction.

Classification 3
System loopholes

Length of time in court: There are tons of cases in the court. Any Indian knows the amount of time and money involved in going to court. In fact, my case lasted a decade and this was at the first level, it could've gone into appeal and perhaps lasted even longer.

I read an interesting article in the *Times of India* where the respondent stated that her divorce case had been going on for over twenty-five years and now the matter was referred to the Supreme Court, so heaven help her. Perhaps they would be still married when they headed for the grave.

Solution and Safety Measures: Be realistic about your case and don't base your life on it. Continue living your life as normally as possible and avoid living from one court date to another.

If possible, try for an out-of-court settlement. It is less expensive and time consuming, both financially and emotionally, and it brings your case to closure faster.

Laxity of law in not throwing out a case or adequate punishment: Usually the judge doesn't dismiss a case very easily and there are more chances given to continue the case. For example, even if the husband has not paid the interim maintenance, the judge gives time for the payment. The husband can also ask for more time and usually if the court feels he has presented adequate reason then they do grant him time. Although I wish the court would not be so lax and provide so many opportunities to continue the case. Yet that is wishful thinking and even if that were to change, it would take a long time before those changes were instituted.

This can be understood with an example. When my friend's husband did not pay her interim maintenance for eight months, ideally his petition should have been dismissed as he had defied a court order. But the law kept giving him more time to pay. He could afford to pay but hadn't paid. The law does confer them with inherent powers for dismissal, however they do not utilize it. In a way, it is carrying the spirit of law to the extreme.

Even the time given for presenting a written statement and other petitions is very long and the court does keep granting more time in case adequate reasoning has been provided. I have seen it not only in my case but also quite a few others. This is very frustrating but like I say, since I can't change this, might as well just put up with it smilingly, to make it easier.

Solution and Safety Measures: Be aware of the recourse to law that you have. For example, if the women haven't been paid, they can file a RD and if they are still not paid, can ask the court to dismiss their spouse's petition and the court will take cognizance.

One has to be aware of the law when you are caught in the midst of it, and nowadays, it is much easier with online help.

Classification 4
Loopholes used by *hum aur tum* (man and woman)

Fake witnesses: This is used by both and these are witnesses who report things that they claim to know about either or both parties and speak ill about one and praise the other. Since the cases are based on personal issues, and no one really knows what goes on in a couple's bedroom, it becomes even more difficult to prove or disprove.

Solution and Safety Measures: You as a party to the case should not produce fake witnesses as they may end up committing perjury.

In many instances you may actually have real witnesses or other documents like letters, communications and sometimes even newspaper clippings (for my case I had paper clippings disproving what they had said) proving your innocence, so use these. Once you can prove a couple of witnesses from the other side to be fakes, their case becomes weak.

Delaying tactics applied in court: This too, coupled with the above, leads to a case carrying on interminably. One side may take longer dates, citing many reasons like the lawyer having another matter and hence not being available on the date decided by the court. Some excuses are considered valid and some are not, but that doesn't stop the party trying to delay the matter to enact every trick in the book to buy time. The judges may accede to the request of the lawyer's unavailability and sometimes even to the fact that the client is travelling for work and may not be able to appear at the given date, hence another date. Sometimes even the judge may be unavailable

Often clients also change lawyers and this again delays the case, though at times this may be legitimate. So a court case takes very long. When you have a court case you realize that patience is truly a virtue.

At times, the judge may not agree for a longer date, but my experience has been that usually the court is accommodating which leads to your frustration. Plus usually the court is so overburdened with cases that you do tend to get longer dates.

Solution and Safety Measures: If there is an

inordinate delay and you want the court to speed up the matter, keep a record of the number of times the opposing side is asking for longer dates and thus delaying the matter. The court will take cognizance of this and try to avoid falling for the delay tactics of the other side.

Frivolous petitions: I am guilty of using these and so is Paneer Boy. These are additional petitions aside from the actual petition and they are added to delay the case as they have to be decided on before the main petition is heard.

Another tactic is filing an appeal against an order in High Court, and since the matter is under appeal it cannot be heard in the lower court.

Solution and Safety Measures: I am afraid I have no advice to counter this.

Changing of facts in petition by having a cleverly drafted examination-in-chief:

Solution and Safety Measures: In case you feel this is the case then you should ensure that the judge takes cognizance and these are struck out. Be alert yourself too and don't be wholly dependent on the lawyer.

Loopholes used by lawyers

Lawyers: Ah! Now let's see what our esteemed friends do in these cases. They may actually not inform you of all the recourses available to you. One support group member was not being paid an interim maintenance and this despite her matter being in court for over four years and she had no clue she was to be paid. In fact, one of my lawyers was handling her case, rather one of my ex-lawyers was handling it. When we intervened, the lawyer very reluctantly filed for it. Sad, because the lawyer wasn't even ashamed about it.

The lawyers also connive with each other to settle cases, which may not always be to their clients' benefit.

They may at times even work against your best interest as the other party has taken care of them.

Some of the lawyers also take care of the police. I visited one such lawyer couple in the family court to ask them to represent me but I was shocked by their demand for a high fee (Rs 50,000 as a retainer, and more to be paid on each meeting, and this was about three years ago). And by their cheapness: 'Get your file xeroxed or we can get it done and put it in your bill.' And yes, the police money you will have to pay separately. God knows whether they were paying the cops or not but they sure as hell were charging their clients for it. I felt however horrible my hubby had been, still he didn't deserve them. So I ran out refusing to drink the dirty water they offered me, probably they would charge me for that too. The funny part is that they are married but she is his second wife, and by law, he isn't permitted to be married twice as he hasn't got a divorce from his first one. Hmm, wonder why he is so scared of divorce himself despite being a divorce lawyer.

I have not cited sections nor legalese in these parts and only provided a general guideline for loopholes that one has to watch out for. Almost no one is ever going to tell you that these exist, especially anyone involved with law. You have to live these to know of their existence.

These are not documented as a separate legal entity, but

are definitely rampant in real life, when your matter is in court. These are documented with help from Taubon Irani, my friends from the support group, and reading countless articles not only in the *Times of India* but other newspapers as well. Most importantly, my experience has helped me to have lived through these loopholes.

I sincerely wish that when I was going through a divorce someone had provided me with the list of these. I am sure I would have had my antennae on red alert. But I didn't do too badly and lived and learnt and I can at least share them with you.

These loopholes will continue to increase as time passes by, quite like the hydra-headed monster.

Appendix 1

In 2011, I heard from a nanny employed by my friend, Lynne. Her name is Diana and was going through a very traumatic relationship with her husband. She wrote to me, telling me her story and asking for my advice. Her initial email is produced below.

★★★

Hi Vandana,

This is Diana and I am the nanny for Lynne's daughter. Lynne told me a lot about you and I am very interested to know more. I will be glad to discuss my problems with you and to get some help in coming out of this situation I need some suggestion from you. I hope you will help me out. This is my email id and I'll really be glad to talk with you.

Her second email was:

I am married to Stan and he is an alcoholic and extremely abusive. I got married at the age of nineteen and it was a love marriage at the church and a registered marriage at Bandra court. I had two kids by the age of twenty-one and was happy with everything. Initially it was like whatever my husband would say was right. But I loved him a lot and after the birth of my kids, it was so bad that I was being hit and abused each and every day. Being a talkative person with a friendly nature, I always had my neighbours and friends around but after marriage all that had stopped because my husband didn't like it.

His abusive behaviour led me to despair and eventually I tried to kill myself when I had no hope left. When I was on the stool with a chunni around my neck, I realized I was relieved to be putting an end to my life. Even though I had two children I still thought that they are better off without seeing me like this. When I pushed the stool, my next door neighbour walked in by chance and got me down from there. Thus my life was saved and I was given a new life.

My husband did not care if I lived or died. In fact, the day I tried to commit suicide he hit me again after I was saved. The bruise marks around my neck gave me both hope and inspiration.

I got a job as a gym instructor and started earning some money. At one stage I was also doing housework for others and earning money so the gym job was a good one especially in comparison to the previous one. Stan would follow me to the gym and once he saw me talking with one of my colleagues, he called the gym and started abusing me. We had a big fight when I returned home.

But still life had to go on. My son, Steven, was deeply affected by all of this. He would behave weirdly in school and from being the topper since his third grade, his rank dropped completely. I got a call from school that my son needs counselling. The counsellor told me that Steven's behaviour was due to the atmosphere at home and she felt really bad for him.

Stan's beatings, abuse and drunken behaviour continued. One day he beat me so much, I thought I had a fracture and then I hit him back. He came at me with a knife and I attacked him with the same knife but then I left him lying there.

My family was of no help because they said that you have to be with your husband and it is your fault if he keeps hitting you. Then one day my aunt took me to the US consulate where they needed a housekeeper. I applied and got the job. From there, because I was good worker, I got a permanent job as a nanny. I didn't tell my husband. But still, Stan would land up and tell my employer that I was a whore and should be thrown out. My employer immediately got him thrown off the premises.

After that, I have continued in my job and finally come to the United States with my employer. He keeps harassing me here too. But my employer is like the family I never had and continues to support and protect me. I am going to study further and make my life. One of my children is in hostel in India and I pay for them to be there. One of them is staying with my sister who I pay for the upkeep. He pays nothing and in fact continues to call me and threaten me. I am not scared anymore but don't want to go back to him. Please help me and guide me.

Thanks,
Diana

Diana isn't still divorced but over the course of three years, I had many counselling sessions with her and exchanged many emails with her. Two of these are produced below.

Email 1:

Diana,
I am glad that you have taken the steps to contact me. I will help you to completely get out of this situation. I'm happy to know that you are working and are financially independent. As regards starting a new life, well, you have already said that you would like to go for a divorce so I will advise you to come and see me. Don't worry about the fee. We will sort that when we meet. After all, your life is at stake.

Please do not meet Stan and stay away from your family that is also on his side and all these are toxic elements in your life.

I'm glad you have started your further education overseas and I am glad you have a supportive employer who is even greater than a family. I hope you find love and the courage to restart a new life soon.

Regards,
Vandana

Email 2:

Hi Diana,

You need to be strong emotionally. I'm happy that you have been working and from what I understand you have also saved a lot of money. Your decision to cut off from Stan, after my advice, is also good since he cannot ask you for either money nor terrorize or threaten you. I gave you this advice after he stole your passport and threatened to tear it. I'm glad you have decided to put both the children in the hostel so that they have a balanced life and are not subjected to his cruelty. Please do remember that these things happen for a purpose and God has his own way of dealing with it. Meditation, as I said earlier, will also help you emotionally. Besides, you are brave and that I have documented in the documentary I have made about your journey.

Regards,
Vandana

Today Diana is successfully studying overseas. She has embraced a new life and is thankful to be alive. She has saved enough to buy a home outside Mumbai. She wants me to be the first person to enter her home because she says that without my advice she would be nowhere. I don't know if it is true but I am glad I have given her a new life.

She hasn't yet filed for divorce because her husband is not agreeable to it. Her children are in the hostel and she continues to do well and thrive. 360 Degrees has helped her to rebuild her life completely.

Appendix 2

The following are three emails among the ones I have received from various people across India and the Middle East who have sought my help while trying to get through their divorces. One of these emails provides an insight into the kind of problems that people face during a divorce and the other two are an acknowledgment of the difference 360 Degrees Back to Life has made to them.

Email dated 17 August 2008

Dear Vandana,
Thanks a million—you made me feel worthwhile again. I just do not know how to express myself. I wish you had come to Muscat and into the limelight much earlier.

I will be in Mumbai in the first week of October and I would like you to give me the opportunity to meet you and make a difference to my life which is going haywire. I really need the moral support of a genius like you.

God bless you always!
Take care and best regards,
Seema

Email 2:

Hi Vandana,

This is Hetal. I read your article 'A New Life' in *She* magazine about divorce and its effects on women. First of all, hats off to you for not only fighting for your rights without the emotional support of your parents but also for starting a divorce support group.

I, too, am a divorcee but by God's grace, I was in a far better position than most other women in similar situations. But still, the emotional trauma remains the same for all women irrespective of their financial status, working status, or support from their parents and relatives. Fortunately I got my divorce in six months as I had foregone my right for maintenance because I was already working and earning well and wanted to come out of that trauma as soon as possible and start my life afresh. Moreover, my parents also were very supportive and helped me a great deal while coming out of this trauma.

I would love it if you could let me know about the divorce support group and its activities and I would be more than happy to be of any help to it.

Waiting to hear from you soon.

Thanks and regards,
Hetal

Email dated 5 May 2008

Hi,

First, let me give my warm wishes to you for doing a great job. I have heard about you from my best friend. To introduce myself, my name is Fatima, and I got married in January 2000 in UP and I am a well-educated female from Mumbai.

Due to my husband's harsh behaviour, conservative mind and insecurity about himself, he started beating me. I came back to my parents' home in December 2000. My husband is a lawyer and practising in Allahabad and his income was not very good. To start earning a living in Mumbai and bring him back with me to Mumbai, I came to my parents' place. But even then, he did not cooperate with me and started writing filthy letters insulting me and my parents, abusing them badly.

In September 2002, I filed a divorce case in Allahabad but as he was a lawyer himself, he could represent himself and fight at the court.

On one court date, he started harassing me in the middle of the road in Allahabad. I was alone that day as my lawyer was not well. That was the first time I couldn't attend the court date and at the next date, the court dismissed my case because I had not attended the previous hearing.

He also filed a case of restitution of conjugal rights which he won ex-parte in April 2007. In response to that, I filed a case for restoration of the case but couldn't win. I thought of filing a fresh case in Mumbai but more than two people advised me to first restore the case in Allahabad and then transfer the case to Mumbai.

Please help me, as my dad is retired and my mom is a housewife and I don't have any idea what to do. Please advise me about what I should do. Thanks for giving me your precious time to read the above matter. Your advice is very valuable.

Thanks,
Mannsha

Acknowledgements

This is the easiest yet toughest part of any project.

I am deeply grateful to Shobhaa Dé, who is my inspiration. I love her for having faith in me to reach the skies and conquer the universe. She helped me take baby steps as a writer, until I could fly on the strength of my words. She is the Queen of Sheeba in every way and we all love her for it.

Professor Nandini Sardesai, my idea of an ideal teacher who has been my guiding light in this quagmire called LIFE. I love you, Ma'am.

Chiki Sarkar, for always being prompt in her responses and always being encouraging.

Milee Ashwarya, who has held my hand when I felt low.

Niyati Dhuldhoya, my editor, who has spent more time with me than her fiancé. I've spent so much time with her that I thought we'd have to start living together.

Paloma Dutta, with the impossibly poetic name, has patiently copy-edited the book. Paloma came in late but is like a cherry atop an ice cream in this effort.

Sunil Doshi, who calls me Cleo, loves me and treats me like an empress. He knows that despite my tantrums I love him right back.

Bobby, who was my angel and protected me like a tigress would protect her cub.

Taubon Irani, who I affectionately call BOSS and who stands beside me like a rock and her fantastic family for accepting me as a part of their lives.

My best friend, Kamaljit Singha, who has smiled with me in good times and bad and bugs me with so many questions about the book that I ended up fine-tuning everything for fear of being grilled.

Abhishek Doshi, who supports me regardless of whether I'm right or wrong and wants to always see me conservatively dressed.

Lekha Menon, my *jaan,* who has helped me so much with the manuscript and read it even though she had so much of her own reading and writing to do.

Arif Zakaria, for going on long walks with me and constantly engaging me in a battle of wits, which always end in a stalemate. But these walks help me write and even though he is a strict disciplinarian and acts pricey with his overdeveloped conscience and talks on morality, he is a yang to my yin to temper my free spirit. He continues to be a solid part of my life and harbours ambitions of seeing me in a burqa. I'd rather be in a burqini and I continue to love him.

Lord Meghnad Desai for guiding my inner voice.

Anil Wadhwa, friend par excellence.

Dr Deshpande, for unflinching support through the years.

Manu Dadlani, for being with me in my toughest times.

Jiten Gajaria, for guiding me in the digital sphere in my work-life.

Dr Sonal Mansingh, for the beauty she brings in my life.

Rafael Nadal for being the constant love and lust of my life, for continuing to increase my belief in myself.

I thank all the members of my support group for being my friends and also my friends who are unnamed but remain in my heart.

I must also thank all my detractors—my beloved relatives, my unsupportive, disapproving brother-in-law, my ex-husband and so many like them who continued their constant attacks, making me respond by flying higher and higher.

Finally, I thank Penguin who, along with Shobhaa Dé, believed in me enough to commission this book. How would it all have come together without them? Thanks guys for your trust. You believed in me more than I believed in myself.